Can
Elephants
Swim?

Can Elephants Swim?

Unlikely Answers to Improbable Questions

◆

Compiled by Robert M. Jones
from the Libraries of TIME-LIFE BOOKS

Illustrated by Stan Mack

TIME-LIFE BOOKS, NEW YORK

Book designed by Herb Quarmby.

© 1969 Time Inc. All rights reserved.
Published simultaneously in Canada.
Library of Congress catalogue card number 73-79769.
School and library distribution by Silver Burdett Company, Morristown, New Jersey.

x

Dedicated to the researchers of
TIME-LIFE BOOKS,
in appreciation of their unending
pursuit of checkable fact

FOREWORD

This book is a snack tray of knowledge, spiced with surprises and delights from every field of human endeavor.

Would you place a bet that Horatio Alger Jr. was a resounding success? (He died poor.) That the skyscraper was born in New York? (Try Chicago.) That Lincoln won the Lincoln-Douglas debates? (Douglas was elected.) That the country with the densest population is in the Orient? (It's in Western Europe.)

Do you really believe that bears hibernate? That all ants are industrious? That birds sing because they are happy? After you read this book you'll know better.

If you are a Renaissance man at heart, a lonely wanderer in an era of specialization, wouldn't it make your day complete to know *for sure* how fast a duck flies? How much water there is in the sea? How old the earth?

And the next time you are trapped at a party by that inevitable bore who knows all about everything, ask him how far a flea can jump. The unlikely answer is right here.

A is for aardvarks, African violets and Horatio Alger

Are aardvarks easy to find?

Despite its size and relative abundance, the aardvark, being nocturnal and confirmedly subterranean, is seldom seen. The name means "earth pig" in Afrikaans, but this 150-pound termite-eating animal has nothing to do with pigs and, except for the tip of its snout, does not look much like one. THE LAND AND WILDLIFE OF AFRICA and THE MAMMALS, LIFE NATURE LIBRARY

What city has the largest African population?

Greater Lagos, the capital of Nigeria, probably has a population of more than a million. The largest urban aggregation of people of African descent, however, is in New York, where Afro-Americans number nearly 1.5 million. In the U.S. as a whole, about 10 per cent of the population descend from Africa—over 20 million people, more than the population of any Tropical African nation except Nigeria. TROPICAL AFRICA, LIFE WORLD LIBRARY

9

What is the chief threat to the *African violet?*

An open window; the African violet does not grow well unless kept warm. It is endangered at temperatures below 65°F., and will die at around 50°F., long before frost is reached.   THE PLANTS. LIFE NATURE LIBRARY

What is the healthiest *age?*

When a child is about five, he enters the most adaptable phase of life, "the golden age of resistance," which continues until he is 15. During these years the mortality rate for nearly every infectious disease is at its lowest. The body's ability to mobilize its forces with precision remains high through the early twenties (nearly all speed records for the 100-yard dash have been set by men who were scarcely out of their teens) and to some extent continues into the thirties. But then this efficiency begins to wane.   HEALTH AND DISEASE, LIFE SCIENCE LIBRARY

How much does *air weigh?*

Insubstantial as it seems, air has ponderous mass. Held to earth by gravity, it has a total weight of at least 5,600 trillion tons. At sea level, a vertical column of air one inch square and extending to the outer reaches of the atmosphere weighs 14.7 pounds; a column a foot square weighs more than a ton. On each human at sea level, depending on his size and the area of his skin surface, the atmosphere exerts a pressure of from 10 to 20 tons. Man survives at the bottom of his sea just as fish survive at the bottom of theirs: inner body pressure, pushing out, equalizes atmospheric pressure, pushing in.   WEATHER. LIFE SCIENCE LIBRARY

How did things go on the first *air-mail flight?*

The first air-mail flight between Washington and Philadelphia in 1918 was a navigational fiasco. President Woodrow Wilson, Postmaster General Albert S. Burleson and other members of the Cabinet gathered near the Washington Monument to witness the takeoff on a perfectly clear day. But the pilot somehow ended up near Waldorf, Maryland, some 20 miles southeast of Washington—and a good hundred air miles from Philadelphia. The mail was unceremoniously removed and sent on by train.

FLIGHT. LIFE SCIENCE LIBRARY

How is *air traffic* controlled?

Airliners fly from city to city along clearly defined airways, numbered aerial highways complete with directional signs, speed limits and traffic patrols. The airways are marked by interlocking radio signals constantly beamed into the sky by ground transmitters along the route. Receivers in the plane pick up these signals and immediately indicate the direction and distance of the station. By checking these with an airways chart, the pilot can fix his exact position with more ease and certainty than a motorist reading a roadside sign.

FLIGHT, LIFE SCIENCE LIBRARY

Is *alcohol* a stimulant?

Alcohol's direct effects on the body seem to be limited strictly to one organ: the brain, which controls the body's other activities. On this organ it acts as a depressant, not as the stimulant it is commonly believed to be. Unlike true stimulants, such as caffeine or amphetamine, alcohol retards rather than accelerates the brain's control mechanisms. Its depressant action, depending on the dose, can cause mild or serious mental disorganization, loss of muscular control (most conspicuous in the inebriate's slurred speech and staggering gait), sleep, coma and even death.

DRUGS, LIFE SCIENCE LIBRARY

How successful was **Horatio Alger?**

"Go Slow and Sure, and prosper then you must /With Fame and Fortune, while you Try and Trust," advised Horatio Alger Jr. in novels like *Luck and Pluck.* Alger wrote more than 100 books tracing the climb to success of clean-cut lads who left home to seek their fortune, but he himself chose a path of pleasure that was neither slow nor sure. He died penniless. THE AGE OF STEEL AND STEAM, THE LIFE HISTORY OF THE UNITED STATES

How do **alligators** nest?

The female American alligator builds her nest by biting off huge mouthfuls of damp vegetable trash and combining them with mud to form a mound that may be six feet wide at its base and a yard high. From 15 to 80 eggs are then laid in a hole scooped out of the top. This is promptly covered with material pulled from the rim and packed down smooth. Unlike most other reptiles, the alligator does not abandon her eggs after laying them but hovers about to guard them from other animals. When it is time to hatch, the baby alligators make faint squeaking sounds, signaling their mother to amble over and help them tear open the mound.

THE REPTILES, LIFE NATURE LIBRARY

How do Andean Indians stand the **altitude** at which they live?

Living at altitudes of up to 17,000 feet, Andean Indians have developed certain physical characteristics that make the most use of the oxygen existing at those heights. Their lungs are bigger than normal, so that they inhale more air with each breath. The circulatory system is modified; the Indian has about two quarts more blood than do lowlanders, and the red blood corpuscles, which carry the oxygen, are considerably bigger. Arms and legs are short, hands and feet small, thus reducing the distance the heart has to pump the blood and also reducing the area exposed to the cold. Finally, the heart itself, which pumps blood and oxygen throughout the body, is larger than normal by almost 20 per cent.

THE ANDEAN REPUBLICS, LIFE WORLD LIBRARY

Who named **America**?

A Florentine merchant and banker named Amerigo Vespucci participated in several expeditions that explored more than two thirds of the eastern coastline of South America. Vespucci's reputation as a serious explorer was to suffer from exaggerated accounts of his achievements. But his claim that he had "arrived at a new land which . . . we observed to be a continent" led the geographer Martin Waldseemüller to propose in 1507 that the newly discovered world be called the "Land of Americus, for Americus its discoverer."

THE NEW WORLD, THE LIFE HISTORY OF THE UNITED STATES

How was **anesthesia** discovered?

The first of four discoverers was Dr. Crawford W. Long of Jefferson, Georgia. His drug was ether. Ether can induce a euphoric feeling of buoyancy as well as unconsciousness, and Long had made its acquaintance through the "ether jags" that were a fad when he was a medical student. During ether parties, Long was evidently not too exhilarated to use his eyes, for he noticed that many of his intoxicated friends became quite insensible to pain. In March 1842, he put his observations to work. He gave a young man ether to breathe and then painlessly removed a tumor from the youth's neck. Long continued to use the drug effectively in his own medical practice, but because he was merely a young country doctor, he was too diffident to report his results to any medical journal.

DRUGS, LIFE SCIENCE LIBRARY

What is the size of the largest *animal* that ever lived?

The biggest whales are bigger than any land animal could be. The largest ever caught was a female blue that measured 113½ feet. It used to be thought that whales weighed about a ton a foot. But British scientists have weighed three large whales piece by piece (there is no way of weighing a sizable whale all at once) and found that the big ones work out to a ton and a half per foot. This means that the record blue probably weighed 170 tons, as much as 2,267 human beings weighing 150 pounds each. A whale can grow to such size because water supports its weight against the pull of gravity.   THE SEA, LIFE NATURE LIBRARY

How do *antlers* differ from *horns*?

The horns of antelopes and the antlers of deer, although comparable in function, differ considerably in structure. Horns, usually possessed by both sexes, are permanent features that continue to grow throughout the animal's life. They consist of bony projections from the skull and are covered with a hard substance known as keratin, which is tougher than bone. Antlers, by contrast, are pure bone and are formed and shed every year. They are normally grown only by male deer, with the exception of reindeer and caribou, whose females have them as well.

THE MAMMALS, LIFE NATURE LIBRARY

Do *ants* post sentries?

Ants seem constantly girded for warfare, and casual observers have thought that they post sentinels to guard their nests and foraging territory. These supposed sentinels are easily recognized: their antennae are laid back, their legs drawn close, their bodies pressed tightly against the earth. They remain motionless for hours. But these are not sentries wisely posted by the nest; they are ants exhibiting a little-known characteristic of ants—their laziness.   THE INSECTS, LIFE NATURE LIBRARY

Why is Iraq an *Arab* country, while neighboring Iran is not?

It is not custom and image that bring unity to the Arab world. Nor is religion the sole binding force; Iran, which is as Moslem as the Arab world, is not a part of it, whereas Lebanon, despite being half Christian and half Moslem, is. The cement that unites the Arabs is the shared language of Arabic. President Gamal Abdul Nasser of Egypt has himself defined an Arab as "anyone whose mother tongue is Arabic." (The Iranians speak Persian.)

THE ARAB WORLD, LIFE WORLD LIBRARY

Where were *Arabic numerals* perfected?

In India, about 500 A.D., the Hindus started using a 10-number (decimal) notation in which each number's position showed what power of 10 it represented, while the empty positions were designated by zeros. From India the new numeration spread west to the Moslem world, and finally, through trading and crusading, it reached the capitals of Christendom about 1100 A.D.

THE UNIVERSE, LIFE NATURE LIBRARY

Where is *Armenia?*

Few peoples have known as many changes of fortune as the Armenians. Located in eastern Anatolia (modern Turkey) and extending eastward into what is now the U.S.S.R., Armenia was in ancient times a buffer kingdom between rival empires. Armenia was frequently invaded—by Assyrians, Persians, Arabs, Greeks and Romans. Withal, the Armenians retained their identity. In the 11th Century, after still more invasions of their homeland, a number of Armenians established a new kingdom on the southern coast of Anatolia. This kingdom in its turn was destroyed in the 14th Century by invaders from Egypt.   TURKEY. LIFE WORLD LIBRARY

Are the Germans pure *Aryan?*

Hitler's notions of race can be consigned to the realm of mythology. North and east Germans may have generally conformed to his "ideal" Germanic type, with blond hair, blue eyes and big limbs. But many were dark and of medium build, and probably a majority of Bavarians and Rhinelanders have dark hair, brown eyes and round skulls. The truth is that the Germans, like all other Europeans, have always been both racially and culturally mixed. There is plenty of Latin stock in the west and Slavic blood in the east.   GERMANY. LIFE WORLD LIBRARY

*How often do **asteroids** strike the earth?*

About 1,500 boulder-sized asteroids strike the earth each year. Tons of tiny specks of star dust settle to earth daily, but full-fledged flying mountains (50,000 tons or more) are thought to strike perhaps once every 10,-000 years on the average. Landing with tremendous force, they gouge out huge craters. The largest astrobleme, or "star-wound," visible on the earth's surface today is the over-a-quarter-billion-year-old Vredefort Ring in the Transvaal, with an eroded granite dome 26 miles wide. This must have been formed by an asteroid a mile in diameter, hitting with the explosive force of a million-megaton bomb.   THE UNIVERSE, LIFE NATURE LIBRARY

*How many people lived in ancient **Athens**?*

During the golden age of Pericles, the population of Athens was about 300,000—smaller than that of present-day Omaha. Yet within a few generations Athens developed thinkers and writers and artists who changed the world forever. Dozens of them are still remembered and revered, each man for some previously unheard-of epochal accomplishment.

GREECE, LIFE WORLD LIBRARY

Who invented the *automobile?*

The man who put the first reliable internal-combustion machine on the road was a German, Karl Benz. The Benz car, which appeared in 1885, was a three-wheeler; its engine was in the rear, behind the single seat, and the body was light, with large, delicately spoked wheels. The one-cylinder, four-stroke engine burned benzine; at maximum speed it turned its shaft 250 revolutions per minute, delivered three fourths of a horse-power, and moved automobile and driver down the road at a stately eight miles per hour.   MACHINES, LIFE SCIENCE LIBRARY

When did the *automobile* really zoom into American life?

The 8,000 cars registered in 1900 were chiefly playthings for the wealthy —cranky open-air affairs subject to a host of ailments. By 1917, there were some 4,700,500 loose on the streets (an increase of more than 58,600 per cent); they were reasonably reliable and reasonably weathertight, and sold, new, for as little as $345, F.O.B. Detroit.

THE PROGRESSIVE ERA, THE LIFE HISTORY OF THE UNITED STATES

What does it cost to operate an *automobile?*

The legendary little old lady who drives her car only on Sunday may think she is being economical; the fact is, she is something of a spend-thrift. Her weekly trip to church may cost her as much as 84 cents per mile —about seven times what she would pay per mile if she, like the average American motorist, drove 10,000 miles a year. The big expense of a car is not in driving it but in owning it. A car driven 10,000 miles a year costs about 12 cents a mile to run. Two thirds of that sum, or eight cents, is in fixed costs (insurance, license, registration fees), which do not change no matter how far the car is driven. These fixed costs remain the same whether the car is wrapped in a plastic sheet in the garage or is out rolling along a highway. Even depreciation—the cost of amortizing the original purchase price of the car—changes only slightly with use.

WHEELS, LIFE SCIENCE LIBRARY

What destroyed the *Aztecs and Inca?*

Far more damaging to Aztec and Inca civilization than Spanish conquest were the invisible microorganisms unwittingly brought from Europe. Pes-tilence after pestilence took a shocking toll among the susceptible Indian population. Some of these devastating epidemics were smallpox, others probably measles and influenza. The cumulative effect of the pestilences was horrible in the extreme. Both the Gulf and Pacific coasts of Mexico were swept almost clear of people. The Valley of Mexico lost about 80 per cent of its Indians by 1600. The same happened in Peru, where the dense populations of the coastal oases practically disappeared. The fer-tile Rimac Valley, where modern Lima stands, lost almost 95 per cent of its people in less than 50 years. ANCIENT AMERICA, GREAT AGES OF MAN

B is for baby faces, bird's-nest soup and bloomers

*Does a **baby face** arouse parental instinct?*

There seems to be evidence that it does. The human baby, the bunny, the puppy and the chick all have features, or sign stimuli, that stir up parental feelings: short faces, prominent foreheads, round eyes, plump cheeks. The angular, elongated faces of adults do not awaken the same feelings. Parental response in humans extends not only toward children but also toward such popular baby substitutes as pets and dolls.

ANIMAL BEHAVIOR, LIFE NATURE LIBRARY

*What language is spoken in the **Balkans?***

There are six major languages in the Balkans: Bulgarian, Macedonian, Serbo-Croatian, Slovenian, Albanian and Romanian. Two of these languages, Bulgarian and Macedonian, exclusively employ the Cyrillic alphabet, which is also used in Russian. Three languages—Slovenian,

Albanian and Romanian—use the Latin alphabet of English. And one language, Serbo-Croatian, can be written with either the Cyrillic or the Latin alphabet, the Serbs using the Cyrillic, the Croats the Latin.

THE BALKANS. LIFE WORLD LIBRARY

What is a *banana republic?*

At the turn of the century, Central America, in popular American thinking, had no reason for existence but the growing of bananas; the nations of Central America were regarded as being in the pockets of U.S. banana growers and, as such, were known as "the banana republics." Even today the name persists—because the image persists.

CENTRAL AMERICA. LIFE WORLD LIBRARY

Could you draw water from a *barrel cactus?*

The legend overstates the fact. To get liquid one must first behead the plant, then mash the pulpy interior until a liquid (unpleasant-tasting at that) is obtained. This is hard, perspiring work, and besides, the barrel cactus bristles with spines so tough and sharp that the Indians used to use them for fishhooks.

THE DESERT. LIFE NATURE LIBRARY

How busy is a *bee?*

In order to fill its honey sac, the average worker bee has to visit between 1,000 and 1,500 individual florets of clover. About 60 full loads of nectar are necessary to produce a mere thimbleful of honey. Nevertheless, during a favorable season, a single hive might store two pounds of honey a day—representing approximately five million individual bee journeys.

THE INSECTS, LIFE NATURE LIBRARY

Why was the *Berlin Wall* built?

The Iron Curtain that divides Germany used to be far from impassable. Nearly three million East Germans poured into West Berlin—their obvious escape route to freedom—or across the borders of the Federal Republic between 1949 and August 1961, when the Berlin Wall was thrown up. Since then the flow of escapees has dwindled to a trickle.

GERMANY. LIFE WORLD LIBRARY

What *bird* is the most numerous on earth?

Of all the world's birds, none has had a more intimate association with man or contributed more to his welfare than the red jungle fowl *Gallus gallus*. From this one species of pheasant, all the many varieties of domestic chickens have had their origin, and today the number of individuals runs into the billions. They are, indeed, far more numerous than the human race. THE BIRDS, LIFE NATURE LIBRARY

How does a *bird* navigate?

At least a part of a bird's ability to navigate appears to depend on its visual perception of landmarks—but only a part. Albatrosses flown by airplane thousands of miles from their Midway Island nests have found their way back over unfamiliar stretches of ocean; one returned after covering more than 4,000 miles in 32 days. Recent experiments have shown that certain species of birds make use of the sun and stars to navigate, and may even possess an "internal clock" capable of making time corrections for the changing position of the sun. FLIGHT, LIFE SCIENCE LIBRARY

*How well can **birds** converse?*

Birds can hear within roughly the same range as man. In some ways they surpass humans: they can hear and respond to the fluctuations in a song about 10 times faster than man. Along with their advanced ears, birds have vocal organs with which to create complex calls. The meadow-lark, for example, has a repertoire of some 50 songs, derived from a "vocabulary" of 300 notes. And the mockingbird is so adept at the use of its vocal cords that it can imitate with remarkable fidelity the calls of many other birds, and even snatches of songs borrowed from humans.

SOUND AND HEARING, LIFE SCIENCE LIBRARY

*How fast do **birds** fly?*

The speed of most small birds seldom exceeds 30 miles per hour, although swallows and particularly starlings are much faster. Migrating hawks cruise along at 30 to 40 miles per hour. Most shore birds average between 40 and 50 miles per hour, while many ducks travel 50 to 60. Blue geese make the 1,700 miles from James Bay in Canada to coastal Louisiana in 60 hours.

THE BIRDS, LIFE NATURE LIBRARY

*What **birds** of different feathers nest together?*

The strange bird called the hoatzin shares with the ibis the same nesting places in the deep jungles on the borders of Colombia and Venezuela, and both birds hatch their young in thorn trees when the rains flood the plains. They differ sharply, however, in survival equipment. If an ibis chick, frightened by some intruder, falls into the water, a shoal of deadly piranha fish quickly pick its bones. Not so the baby hoatzin. At a sign of danger, the chick drops into the water, where, protected by a piranha-repellent odor, it lies submerged until the enemy moves on. Then it uses the unique claws that are attached to its wings to climb back up the tree into its nest.

COLOMBIA AND VENEZUELA AND THE GUIANAS, LIFE WORLD LIBRARY

*Do **birds** sing because they are happy?*

Sentimentalists who like to think that avian melodies are hymns of joy find it hard to believe that they are more generally announcements of status—tough talk to rivals. The vast majority of bird songs are produced by males and break down to two kinds: first, a call from male to male, proclaiming territory and warning other males away, and second, a call to females, advertising the singer's maleness if he is not already committed.

THE BIRDS, LIFE NATURE LIBRARY

What are the extremes in the sizes of **birds' nests?**

Just which birds make the smallest nests and which the largest is a matter of dispute. Some hummingbirds build nests scarcely an inch in diameter, but just as small is the tiny saucer of bark, down and dried glue in which the crested tree swift fits its single egg. At the other extreme, a famous bald eagle nest at Vermillion, Ohio, measured eight and a half feet in diameter and 12 feet in depth, and weighed two tons. Another supernest—this one built by a pair of eagles near St. Petersburg, Florida—had a diameter of nine and a half feet and a depth of 20.

THE BIRDS, LIFE NATURE LIBRARY

What is **bird's-nest soup** made of?

Delicious bird's-nest soup is actually made from the nests of the little cave swiftlets of the Indo-Australasia region. These birds use more saliva than other swifts in building nests, and two kinds build their little bracketlike saucers entirely of this agglutinate material. Tremendous numbers of swiftlets colonize some of the limestone caverns along the coast of Indochina, and here men reap their odd harvest with long poles, knocking down fresh nests that have taken more than a month to build.

THE BIRDS, LIFE NATURE LIBRARY

Do **blind people** develop supernormal senses?

The handicapped show us how rich our senses really are. It is not true, for example, that the blind develop supernormal touch. All human beings have high concentrations of nerve endings in the fingertips, lips and tip of nose—sufficient to feel every dot of Braille. But the blind have an urgent motive for developing their perceptions of the fine messages these areas can send. Similarly, their skill in avoiding obstacles comes from their acute perception of echoes bouncing off objects as they approach— echoes that every normal ear picks up but that most people ignore as distractions.

THE MIND, LIFE SCIENCE LIBRARY

How did **bloomers** get their name?

Amelia Jenks Bloomer founded a publication called *Lily* in 1849, crowding it with lively pieces exposing unjust marriage laws and espousing women's rights to higher education and the vote. Mrs. Bloomer became the first American woman to be named a deputy postmaster, but what boomed the circulation of *Lily* and brought her lasting notoriety were her views on dress reform—the tight bodice, short skirt and full trousers soon known as "bloomers." She wore this garb for a number of years, drawing large crowds wherever she talked and shocked attention wherever she walked. THE SWEEP WESTWARD. THE LIFE HISTORY OF THE UNITED STATES

What part of the human **body** is water?

The amount of water in the body, averaging 65 per cent, varies considerably from person to person. A lean man may have as much as 70 per cent of his weight in the form of body water, while a woman, because of her larger proportion of water-poor fatty tisses, may be only 52 per cent water. WATER. LIFE SCIENCE LIBRARY

Can *body sensitivity* predict storms?

Some people appear to have a sixth sense about a coming storm: it seems to function with special sharpness in the aged, the allergic, the overweight, the chronically ill and the hypersensitive. They feel it in their bones, their joints, their muscles, their sinuses, the palpitations of their hearts. Imagination? Not necessarily. Scientists have detected measurable changes within the body that correspond to changes in atmospheric pressure—especially in the old, infirm and emotionally unstable, whose biological processes may be unusually sensitive. Changes in pulse and respiration rates, blood pressure, blood composition and various other physical processes systematically reflect the transit of the low-pressure and high-pressure air masses that regularly precede and follow the storm.

WEATHER, LIFE SCIENCE LIBRARY

How much do *bones* add to body weight?

Bone is amazingly strong and at the same time amazingly light. In a 160-pound man only about 29 pounds—less than 20 per cent—represent bone weight. Steel bars of comparable size would weigh at least four or five times as much. THE BODY. LIFE SCIENCE LIBRARY

How many **bones** does the human body contain?

A mature body contains 206 bones, not counting the tiny sesamoid bones —like sesame seeds—embedded in the tendons of the thumb, big toe and other pressure points. The figure represents a comedown; newborn babes may have more than 300. By adulthood many of these bones have fused. Not infrequently, however, fusion fails. An otherwise average person may find himself with an extra bone in the arch of the foot, and one in every 20 people has an extra rib. This appendage appears three times as often in men as in women—possibly a form of compensation for the rib Adam yielded up to Eve. THE BODY. LIFE SCIENCE LIBRARY

What is the secret of **bonsai?**

In this Japanese art of growing dwarf trees—cherry trees, cedars, maples —every possible trick is used to inhibit the growth of the plants. In their natural state all would be many feet high, but they are carefully deprived of nutrients, pruned of their fastest-growing shoots and buds, and kept in small pots with reduced root systems. They respond by turning into miniatures of themselves, with tiny leaves and twisted little trunks— their growth almost, but not quite, brought to a standstill. The smaller and more gnarled their trunks and the more tortuous their branches, the more effectively they suggest age and the more highly they are prized. Some of these stunted trees are centuries old. THE PLANTS. LIFE NATURE LIBRARY

What is the second-most-reprinted **book** in the world?

At the age of 50, under the weight of discouragement, Don Miguel de Cervantes Saavedra—a threadbare old man who had been in jail for debt and was finally ready to accept his own mediocrity—sat down to write an amusing short story and ended up producing the greatest masterpiece of Spanish literature. All the ingredients for his work were at hand —the picaresque, the pastoral, the groundwork of literary realism, the national epic poem of the ideal—and Cervantes drew them all together in *Don Quixote de La Mancha,* a book that has been reprinted more often than any other volume except the Bible. SPAIN. LIFE WORLD LIBRARY

*In what country are the most **books** printed?*

Despite the illiteracy of the past, Russian authors have always enjoyed a large, avid and attentive audience, which the Kremlin's mass-education drive has further enlarged. Nowhere today are books printed in such quantities as in the Soviet Union. In the Moscow subway one often finds half the passengers immersed not in newspapers or popular magazines but in copies of the works of such authors as Turgenev, Chekhov and Pushkin.

RUSSIA, LIFE WORLD LIBRARY

*Who were the first **bootleggers?***

Before Prohibition, bootleggers were simply those who hid whiskey in their bootlegs. But from 1920 to 1933 the term covered everyone dealing in illegal alcohol—a traffic that exceeded 70 million gallons each year. WAR, BOOM AND BUST, THE LIFE HISTORY OF THE UNITED STATES

*How does a drab **bowerbird** attract a mate?*

Instead of wooing with a proud display of finery, a bowerbird entices a mate by building and decorating a courting area. The plainer the bowerbird, the more elaborate the bower is likely to be. The dull-hued Lauterbach often uses more than 3,000 sticks in the construction of its love nest, piles perhaps 1,000 pebbles against the walls and embellishes the bower daily with berries. The satin bowerbird shows a preference for blue; it often uses its beak to paint the bower with charcoal, chewed bark and saliva. EVOLUTION, LIFE NATURE LIBRARY

Where do Brazil nuts come from?

The rich nut of the *Bertholletia excelsa* is abundant in northern Bolivia, but because it could be more easily exported by way of Brazil it became known in world markets as the Brazil nut. THE ANDEAN REPUBLICS, LIFE WORLD LIBRARY

Where did the Br'er Rabbit stories originate?

Br'er Rabbit is a variation of a basic folklore character brought to the West Indies by African slaves in their Anansi stories. Anansi is a spider whose origin is buried in prehistory; in Gold Coast mythology, he appeared as creator of the world and stealer of the sun, but by the time he reached the West Indies he was a trickster who generally managed to triumph even though he tangled with such powerful foes as tigers. He is recognizable as Brer Nancy in Jamaica, Ti Malice in Haiti and B'Rabby in the Bahamas, and in the southern United States he became Br'er Rabbit, whose adventures were recorded in the Uncle Remus stories by Joel Chandler Harris.

THE WEST INDIES, LIFE WORLD LIBRARY

Where was **bubonic plague** first controlled?

When the Black Death roamed Europe in the 14th Century, one physician, Balvignus, warned his fellow Jews in the ghetto near Strasbourg to burn their refuse and observe sanitary practices. They did, and the rats, which carry the common fleas that transmit the plague, deserted the Jewish quarter. The result: the death rate in the ghetto during the epidemic was only 5 per cent of that in the rest of the community.

THE CELL, LIFE SCIENCE LIBRARY

How extensively did the **buffalo** roam?

When Columbus discovered America, the boundaries of buffalo country stretched from New York to Oregon and into Canada and Mexico. By 1906 the wild buffalo grounds had dwindled to two tiny areas in Yellowstone Park and near Canada's Lake Athabasca. ECOLOGY, LIFE NATURE LIBRARY

Where were the first **bungalows** built?

The type of one-story building with a veranda known as a bungalow was first built in India. The word derives from the Hindi *bangla*, meaning "belonging to Bengal." INDIA, LIFE WORLD LIBRARY

How far can a **butterfly** fly?

The North American monarch butterfly, often called "the wanderer," is capable of long flights at speeds of 20 miles an hour or more. It produces as many as four generations a year, each of which ventures a little farther north. The last migrates before the oncoming of winter. From as far north as Canada, swarms of butterflies begin gathering from their homes in the fields, clinging to trees and bushes by the thousands. Then, on just the right breeze, they rise in a red cloud and head south. Monarchs have been observed within 200 miles of the coast of England, although not native to Europe. THE FOREST, LIFE NATURE LIBRARY

C is for California, cats, and corned beef and cabbage

What is *calculus* good for?

When the great 17th Century mathematicians Isaac Newton and Gottfried Wilhelm von Leibniz developed calculus as a way of measuring motion, they were, in a sense, introducing to mathematics the principle of the motion picture. For just as a movie film consists of repeated still pictures of a moving object, so does calculus break motion down into "stills" that can be observed "frame by frame." Once calculus was invented, mathematicians could treat a moving object as a point tracing a path through space and, by "stopping the action," calculate the object's speed and acceleration at a specific instant. MATHEMATICS, LIFE SCIENCE LIBRARY

How did *California* get its name?

The white man named California before he saw it. In 1535, the Spanish conquistador Hernán Cortés visited the tip of what is now Baja California, in Mexico. The coastline of that rugged peninsula evoked for him images of an imaginary Indies island described in a popular Spanish novel of the time. Ruled by a black Amazon named Calafía, the fictional island possessed only one metal: gold. By the time Juan Rodríguez Cabrillo stepped ashore for Spain in San Diego Bay on September 28, 1542, to become the first European on California soil, that entire stretch of the Pacific coast had derived its name from that of the legendary black Queen.

THE PACIFIC STATES, TIME-LIFE LIBRARY OF AMERICA

Why does a *camel* have a *hump?*

The camel's hump is made up mostly of fat, accumulated when both food and water are available. During shortages, the animal draws upon this fat, whose hydrogen molecules combine with inhaled oxygen to form water. Prolonged dehydration makes the camel lean, but it can go on functioning efficiently. When supplied with water it begins to resume its normal shape, often consuming over 25 gallons in a few minutes.

THE DESERT, LIFE NATURE LIBRARY

Which big cat makes the best pet?

Although the cheetah is the quintessence of dynamic ferocity in attacking its prey, it is by far the most easily tamed of the big cats. The fully grown male seldom develops the tendency to the sudden fits of annoyance that make leopards so disappointing to people who rear them from their cuddly cubhood and then suddenly find themselves attacked for their pains.   THE LAND AND WILDLIFE OF AFRICA, LIFE NATURE LIBRARY

How fast can a cheetah run?

The cheetah is the champion sprinter of the animal kingdom, overtaking its prey of swift gazelles and antelopes in half-mile bursts. A cheetah was clocked at 20 seconds over a distance of more than 700 yards—averaging just over 71 miles an hour, a record for mammals. Still more remarkable are its powers of acceleration, which can take it from a standing start to 45 miles per hour in two seconds—a performance that cannot be approached by even the fastest racing cars.   THE MAMMALS, LIFE NATURE LIBRARY

What is the population of China?

China has by far the largest population of any country in the world—considerably more than 700 million people. At least one out of every five persons on earth is Chinese.   CHINA, LIFE WORLD LIBRARY

When was China a great naval power?

Between 1405 and 1433 the Ming emperors sent seven maritime expeditions probing down into the South Seas and across the Indian Ocean. The Ming fleets, with as many as 62 huge ships and 28,000 men, were the most powerful task forces the world had ever seen. They made China feared and respected from Sumatra to the east coast of Africa.

CHINA, LIFE WORLD LIBRARY

How did Thoreau exercise civil disobedience?

Henry Thoreau formed the perfect state (population: one) on the shores of Walden Pond in Concord, where he lived in isolation for 26 months. He declined to pay taxes to a national state that permitted slavery—and if this meant doing without the post office, he said, that suited him, as he could think of little news that he cared to receive from the post office anyhow. THE SWEEP WESTWARD, THE LIFE HISTORY OF THE UNITED STATES

Where was the *clipper ship* born?

Early in the 19th Century faster vessels were wanted to run from prowling European men-of-war, to do a little smuggling or privateering, or to engage in the slave trade. Chesapeake Bay shipbuilders, in particular, experimented with handy, fast, small ships and soon developed a schooner known as the "Virginia pilot boat," or the "Virginia model," which, with minor refinements, became in the 1820s the famous Baltimore clipper and, ultimately, the Yankee clipper, romantic symbol of the windships' final era. The word "clipper," American in origin, is believed to derive from "clip" in the sense of speed, as in "to move at a fast clip."

SHIPS, LIFE SCIENCE LIBRARY

Do they really grow a lot of *coffee* in Brazil?

For many years coffee has been Brazil's best-known product, its greatest item of export and its biggest source of income. During the 1960s Brazilian coffee growers produced as much as one third of the world's coffee each year—all stemming from some shoots stolen by a lone Brazilian from a French plantation in French Guiana in the early 18th Century.

BRAZIL, LIFE WORLD LIBRARY

In coin tossing, what are the odds on heads or tails?

Tossing a coin is an exercise in probability theory that everyone has tried: calling either heads or tails is a fair bet because the chance of either result is one half. No one expects a coin to fall heads once in every two tosses, but in a large number of tosses the results tend to even out. For a coin to fall heads 50 consecutive times, a million men would have to toss coins 10 times a minute and 40 hours a week—and then it would happen only once every nine centuries.

MATHEMATICS, LIFE SCIENCE LIBRARY

Who owns a Communist collective farm?

In Eastern Europe, there are three kinds of farms: state, collective and private. On a state farm, which is the preferred type according to Marxist doctrine, the state owns the land, and the workers are paid fixed salaries. On a collective farm, members contribute land to join, retain ownership of

it, and are remunerated in both money and produce according to the
work performed and the results achieved. EASTERN EUROPE, LIFE WORLD LIBRARY

What is the oldest college in the U.S.?

Alumni of Oxford and Cambridge Universities founded the Boston Latin School in 1635 and a college in 1636. Two years later the college was
named for a benefactor, John Harvard. THE NEW WORLD, THE LIFE HISTORY OF THE UNITED STATES

Do animals see colors?

Dogs, horses, cattle, deer and, in fact, most mammals see no colors at
all; everything they look at is perceived in shades of gray. Most birds
and probably some fishes do see some colors. Only apes and higher mon-
keys share man's full color vision. THE CELL, LIFE SCIENCE LIBRARY

How big is a comet?

By the time a good-sized comet has crossed the orbit of Jupiter, the
cloud surrounding its nucleus—called a head, or coma—is big enough
to be seen with a telescope. As the comet plunges nearer the sun, more
gas evaporates, taking some of the dust along into space. The head
swells enormously, sometimes exceeding 100,000 miles in diameter, and
a brilliant tail begins to extend in the direction away from the sun.
Sometimes the tail of a large comet is as much as 50 million miles long.

PLANETS, LIFE SCIENCE LIBRARY

Did communism ever exist peacefully in the U.S.?

Numerous "communistic" groups existed in the industrial and intellectual ferment of 19th Century America. Inspirationists, Shakers, Perfectionists, Mormons—all across the country a great array of hopeful utopians established communities, each avowedly communistic in its pooling of resources and earnings for the good of all. This was not, of course, Communism as later generations would know it. The militant international movement of Karl Marx and Friedrich Engels, with its emphasis on class war and revolution, did not yet exist.

THE SWEEP WESTWARD, THE LIFE HISTORY OF THE UNITED STATES

*Why wasn't the original **Communist Revolution** suppressed?*

Four factors prevented the defeat of what was originally a pitifully weak Bolshevik government in Russia: the divided leadership of the White Russian troops; the failure of the White Russians to arouse popular backing; growing Russian suspicion of all foreign intervention; and finally, the Red Army's strategic position at the core of the country's transportation network.

RUSSIA, LIFE WORLD LIBRARY

*Do **continents** float?*

The idea that a continent—or indeed any major land mass, such as a large island—floats on the earth's mantle is known as the theory of isostasy. A direct verification of the theory is found in the fact that the entire Scandinavian Peninsula is rising in the air. Pressed down by the weight of glaciers years ago, Scandinavia is now believed to stand nearly a thousand feet higher than it did under the burden of the icecap, and parts of it are currently going up at the rate of three feet a century. Some estimates indicate it still has about 650 feet to go before it reaches equilibrium.

THE EARTH, LIFE NATURE LIBRARY

*Is **corned beef and cabbage** a favorite dish in Ireland?*

Contrary to the American impression, it is seldom eaten in Ireland; it became popular among low-paid Irish immigrants in Boston, New York and Chicago before the turn of the century because corned beef was selling in America then for five cents a pound.

IRELAND, LIFE WORLD LIBRARY

*How true to life is the **cowboy** legend?*

Though the danger from Indians and rustlers was later overrated by ro-
mancers, the cowpoke with his spurs a-jingling did carry a gun as the tri-
umphant symbol of his right to make and enforce his own code of
behavior. He did wear picturesquely functional clothes—broad-brimmed
hat against the sun, work gloves for handling reins all day, chaps to protect legs from tangling with brush, high-heeled boots to anchor him in
his stirrups. But in retrospect he became not simply an employee who
got a dollar a day, plus beans and bacon, for exhausting work; he was en-
shrined as the mounted man who rode free—tough, alone and unmarred
by civilization.   THE AGE OF STEEL AND STEAM, THE LIFE HISTORY OF THE UNITED STATES

*How sacred are **cows** in India?*

The Hindu veneration for the cow dates back at least 3,000 years and
may have originated partly as a practical measure to protect the supply
of milk. Eventually the custom became ingrained in religious tradition.
Cows are not actually worshipped as deities in India, and many of them
are not especially well treated. In practice the veneration takes the form
of an absolute prohibition against killing a cow.   INDIA, LIFE WORLD LIBRARY

38

Are *crocodiles* dangerous?

A number of the bigger crocodilians are perversely unable to see the special nature of the human animal and absent-mindedly eat him from time to time. The South American caiman, a relative of the mild-mannered American alligator, is bad this way, and so is the salt-water crocodile of Asia. The worst is no doubt the classic Nile crocodile, chiefly because of an almost ritual indifference on the part of women who wash clothes along East African lakes and rivers. They not only wash there, under the rapt gaze of cruising crocodiles, but actually face the peril rear-end-to, clinging stubbornly to the ancestral custom of standing in the water and scrubbing the wash on a rock on the bank. It is folly to think a crocodile would ignore such an invitation; often they do not.

THE REPTILES, LIFE NATURE LIBRARY

Is *Cro-Magnon* cave art rare?

No—there are more than 70 sites of Cro-Magnon cave art in France alone. These date from approximately 28,000 to 10,000 B.C.

EARLY MAN, LIFE NATURE LIBRARY

How many *Currier & Ives* prints were published?

Nathaniel Currier and James Merritt Ives both liked horses, fires, art and profits. Currier & Ives flourished in the 19th Century, publishing some 7,000 prints—more than all competitors combined. From the five-story factory where artists painted, men printed and women hand-colored pictures, prints went out across the nation and to Europe. Prints were cheap: from five to 25 cents apiece. In America they appeared everywhere, especially in homes, bars, barber shops and hotels.

REACHING FOR EMPIRE, THE LIFE HISTORY OF THE UNITED STATES

Is a *cyclone* destructive?

Cyclones are the familiar "lows" of the weather map, the *bringers* of bad weather—clouds, rainstorms, blizzards; they are *not* synonymous with the violent windstorms so often mistakenly associated with their name. Anticyclones are the weather map's "highs," and normally bring good weather.
WEATHER, LIFE SCIENCE LIBRARY

D is for Democratic Party, dodos and doldrums

How Danish is **Danish trout**?

The Danes have an undisputed genius for marketing. Although the country has almost no trout streams, Danish trout has captured much of the American frozen market. The Danes raise the fish in artificial ponds.

SCANDINAVIA, LIFE WORLD LIBRARY

Where did **democracy** originate?

Democratic government began with the ancient Greeks, though their concept of democracy was far more limited than ours. They had slaves, and no slave, woman or child was considered a citizen. But while the Greeks heeded law and prized order, they also had a passion for freedom and abhorred corruption and tyranny. Aristophanes could denounce in a play an officeholder as "this public robber, this yawning gulf of plunder, this devouring Charybdis, this villain, this villain, this villain." And according to the law: "If anyone rise up against the people with a view to tyranny . . . whoever kills him . . . shall be blameless." No citizen was barred from office, and in Athens most served at some time because many positions were filled by lot. The word democracy itself derives from the Greek *dēmos*, meaning people. CLASSICAL GREECE, GREAT AGES OF MAN

When was the **Democratic Party** born?

The 1828 campaign for the Presidency was underway almost before the John Quincy Adams Administration had begun in 1825. The nation's one party (Republican) split in two. The Adams-Clay group became the National Republicans, later known as the Whigs, and the Jacksonians emerged as the Democratic Republicans, later called the Democrats. The Jackson men resolved that "the sovereign will of the people" was not to be set aside again. For Jacksonians the contest of democracy versus aristocracy had begun. THE GROWING YEARS, THE LIFE HISTORY OF THE UNITED STATES

What are the best defenses against **desert heat**?

U.S. Army research has indicated that desert troops are most efficient when neither overdressed nor stripped down. They should be well clad in lightweight fabrics that are porous, yet dense enough to keep out the sun. Troops can be conditioned to withstand long marches and hard labor in desert heat—so long as they have adequate drinking water. Road gang and oil field workers in the French Sahara get a daily allotment of two gallons of water per man for drinking and cooking alone.

THE DESERT, LIFE NATURE LIBRARY

What is the best **diet** for losing weight?

For a healthy person there is only one remedy for excess weight: a low-calorie diet combined with exercise. This combination, by supplying less energy-producing food than the body uses, reverses the process by which the fat was acquired in the first place. For when the body has used the energy that has been made available by eating, it will turn to its fat storehouse, making gradual withdrawals until all of the excess has been burned off and body weight has returned to normal. Any diet is a good reducing diet provided it is low in calorie value and nutritionally balanced.

FOOD AND NUTRITION, LIFE SCIENCE LIBRARY

What causes *disease?*

Few diseases have only one cause. Thousands of people carry within them the microbes of influenza, tuberculosis, staphylococcus infections and many other illnesses, but this single factor does not make them develop the disease. However, inclement weather or starvation or even a family quarrel may provide the trigger that makes the disease flare up. Every illness, no matter what its nature, is usually the consequence of a variety of causes, not just one—and no two people react to any one cause the same way.   HEALTH AND DISEASE, LIFE SCIENCE LIBRARY

Can *diseases* actually be cured by fake medicines?

Seemingly miraculous cures are often worked by placebos, prescriptions that, according to any scientific criterion, are utterly worthless. The word placebo comes from the Latin verb meaning "to please" and is classically defined as any medicine adapted to benefit the patient by pleasing him. It has been demonstrated on countless occasions that a placebo, a "medicine" containing harmless and inactive ingredients, can relieve anxiety and tension and alleviate pain—even the acute discomfort from major surgery. Moreover, it can cause or cure nausea or diarrhea, reduce stomach acidity, even "cure" the common cold.   DRUGS, LIFE SCIENCE LIBRARY

Why was a baseball team named the **Dodgers?**

During the late 1800s, New York's swift-moving streetcars caused fear, prompting the imaginative people of Brooklyn to call themselves "trolley dodgers" and thus to give a name to their celebrated baseball team, now residents of Los Angeles.   THE GATEWAY STATES, TIME-LIFE LIBRARY OF AMERICA

How did the **dodo** become extinct?

The dodo of Mauritius went so early, so fast and so completely that its name has come to serve the language as a metaphor in conjuring up the idea of obsolescence or goneness—so much so that some people think of the bird as a beast out of somebody's mythology. The dodo was real enough—it was first seen by Europeans when Mauritius was discovered in 1507. One hundred and seventy-four years later the last dodo died. Two factors worked to wipe it out: direct depredation by man (dodos were big, easily caught and fair eating) and changes in the sequestered environment in which its impractical physique had been allowed to evolve.

THE LAND AND WILDLIFE OF AFRICA, LIFE NATURE LIBRARY

What are the **doldrums?**

A theoretical line called the heat equator girdles the globe through its hottest points. On both sides of this shifting line lies the region known since sailing-ship days as the doldrums but which meteorologists call the "intertropical convergence zone." The air over the doldrums has very little horizontal movement—the sun's blazing heat lifts it almost straight up.

WEATHER, LIFE SCIENCE LIBRARY

Are all **dolphins fish?**

Though they look like fish, dolphins of the order Cetacea are true mammals; they are warm-blooded, breathe air and nurse their young. Recent studies of their learning ability suggest that they are extremely intelligent.

THE MAMMALS, LIFE NATURE LIBRARY

*What is the second-largest architectural **dome** in the world?*

Rising above the factories in Providence, Rhode Island, is one of the most handsome state capitol buildings in the U.S. It is built of white marble and has a huge dome exceeded in size only by the one on St. Peter's in Rome.   NEW ENGLAND, TIME-LIFE LIBRARY OF AMERICA

*How did Grover Cleveland avoid the **draft**?*

Grover Cleveland was a poor lawyer when the Civil War began; while two brothers served, he hired a substitute so he could support his mother. In 1884, running for President, he was attacked as a draft dodger. But his backers had a ready answer; his opponent, James G. Blaine, had hired a substitute too. John D. Rockefeller, just starting his sensational business career in 1861, also hired a substitute—although not the 20 or 30 he later boasted of.   THE UNION RESTORED, THE LIFE HISTORY OF THE UNITED STATES

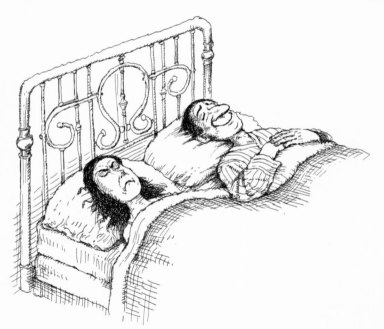

*Does everyone **dream** every night?*

One third of our life is passed in sleep, one fifth of our sleep in dreaming. Science knew little of this constant night life of the brain until, in the

1950s, investigators at the University of Chicago found that sleepers periodically make rapid eye movements. When subjects were wakened during such movements, they testified that they had been dreaming. Further research has shown that everyone dreams. Episodes of dreaming regularly occur for all, about every 90 minutes throughout the night. The episodes become longer during the night, while the depth of sleep, as measured by brain waves, decreases. In eight hours of sleep, the last and longest interlude may be as long as 45 minutes.   THE MIND. LIFE SCIENCE LIBRARY

Is *dried milk* a *modern product?*

As long ago as the 13th Century, men were using dried food that could be reconstituted in somewhat the same way modern milk powder is. The nomadic warriors of Genghis Khan, who spent long hours on horseback, sun-dried mare's milk to a lightweight powder and put some of the powder in a water-filled saddle bottle at the beginning of each day's journey. Stirred throughout the day by the jogging of the horse, the mixture became a thin porridge by nightfall.   FOOD AND NUTRITION. LIFE SCIENCE LIBRARY

What *drug* is *most widely used?*

The most widely used drug in the world is not aspirin, or penicillin, or any other substance commonly prescribed by physicians. It is a material of only minor medical importance, yet it is consumed daily by tens of millions of people, sometimes in dangerous quantities, and on occasion by hundreds of millions more. Indeed, a large majority of the world's people have probably partaken of it, or will partake of it, at some time during their lives. This drug is a colorless, volatile liquid known to the chemist as ethanol, or ethyl alcohol, but to almost everybody else it is simply alcohol.   DRUGS. LIFE SCIENCE LIBRARY

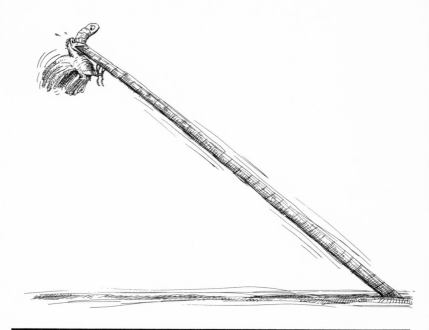

E is for earthworms, elephants and the Establishment

How old is the earth?

The oldest known rocks are represented by some granite gneiss found near Dodoma, Tanzania, with an approximate age of 3.4 billion years. Radioactive-dating studies have been made of meteorite fragments, giving age estimates as great as 4.5 billion years for these bits of solar-system debris. Since it is generally assumed that all of the solar system came into being at the same time, most geologists are prepared to accept this as a figure for the earth's age. THE EARTH, LIFE NATURE LIBRARY

What shape is the earth?

For centuries scientists have thought of the earth as an oblate spheroid—a sphere slightly flattened at the ends, like an orange. Now it develops that it has something of a pear shape as well. A remarkable discovery stemming from the flight of Vanguard I in 1958 has proved that the earth is narrower on top and wider at the hips than had been believed. Although these bulges are barely perceptible, the difference is enough to be scientifically significant. MAN AND SPACE, LIFE SCIENCE LIBRARY

Who first calculated the circumference of the *earth*?

The size of the earth was determined by the Greek mathematician Eratosthenes in 240 B.C., 17 centuries before Magellan first circumnavigated it. From shadow angles, he reckoned the distance from Syene, Egypt, to Alexandria to be ⅕₀ the earth's circumference. Multiplication produced a figure of 25,000 miles for the earth's girth, correct within 100 miles. SHIPS, LIFE SCIENCE LIBRARY

How thick is the crust of the *earth*?

It is a thin layer of rock rarely more than 40 miles thick. It bears about the same relationship to the total bulk of the earth that the shell of an egg bears to the egg. THE MOUNTAINS, LIFE NATURE LIBRARY

How large are the *earthworms* of Australia?

Their size is breathtaking. Some measure a couple of yards long when contracted and as much as 10 feet long when they are extending themselves. THE LAND AND WILDLIFE OF AUSTRALIA, LIFE NATURE LIBRARY

How common are *eclipses*?

A solar eclipse occurs when the moon passes directly between the sun and the earth, while a lunar eclipse takes place when the moon passes through the earth's shadow. Each year, there are at least two eclipses of the sun and maybe as many as five, although most are partial eclipses in which only a segment of the sun's face is covered. Lunar eclipses occur just as often and are seen over larger areas, although some are so faint that they can only be detected with instruments. THE EARTH, LIFE NATURE LIBRARY

How did public *education* start in the U.S.?

The same Oxford and Cambridge alumni who founded Harvard forced the passage of the great Massachusetts school laws of 1642 and 1647.

The 1642 act set fines for parents who failed to teach their children how to read. The 1647 act required every town of 50 families to appoint a schoolteacher, and towns of 100 families to set up a grammar school where children could be educated for Harvard.

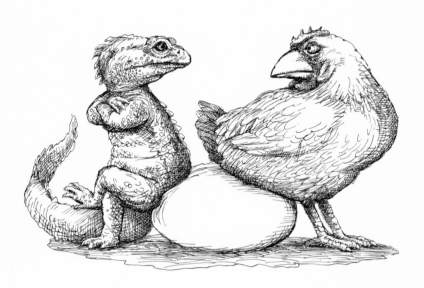

Which came first, the chicken or the egg?

Most people, thinking of an egg, think of a bird; but they are being led astray by seeing eggs mainly at breakfast. The birds did not invent the shelled egg, they inherited it, and it has undergone no important evolution in their possession. The first shelled land eggs were reptilian, and the reptiles were reptiles only when they had evolved such an egg. Applied to reptiles the question of which came first is valid, and paleontologists are still getting testy with each other trying to answer it.

How many eggs does a fish lay?

Nature has ways of making sure that at least enough young survive to perpetuate the race. Special protection may be provided for the egg and young, or the eggs may be produced in such vast numbers that no matter what may befall them some at least are sure to survive. Fish, in most cases, have adopted the second alternative. Eggs are shed into the water in staggering quantities and simply left to the mercy of the environment. A 54-pound ling once caught carried 28,361,000 eggs; a 17-pound turbot had nine million. The cod regularly deposits between four and six million eggs at a single spawning—if they all survived it would take only a few years to pack all the world's oceans tight with codfish.

THE FISHES, LIFE NATURE LIBRARY

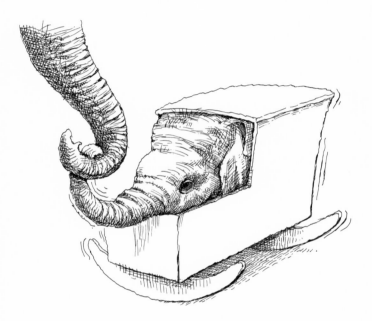

What sort of child psychology is practiced by **elephants?**

Elephant babies are big at birth—about 200 pounds—and grow rapidly into playful and sometimes disobedient youngsters. While on the march, a mother tries to bring her offspring into line with a slap and, if that proves ineffective, may uproot a bush and switch the rebel over the back. But she is also extremely gentle and solicitous. With her all-purpose trunk, she bathes the baby, pushes it up steep embankments and even carries it across streams. Seldom does the youngster leave her side until it is about two years old, because of the danger from marauding lions. In her lifetime of 40 to 50 years, a single cow produces a dozen or more young—most of which stay with "the family" until their teens.

THE LAND AND WILDLIFE OF AFRICA, LIFE NATURE LIBRARY

Can elephants swim?

Some mammals, normally land dwellers, can take to the water quite successfully in special circumstances. Unlikely as it may seem, even elephants are excellent swimmers if the need arises.   THE MAMMALS, LIFE NATURE LIBRARY

Could you sell an icebox to an Eskimo?

The Eskimos often buy refrigerators—which they use to keep food from freezing.   CANADA, LIFE WORLD LIBRARY

What is Britain's Establishment?

The Establishment comprises those influential persons who seem—at least to their detractors—to dominate the political and cultural life of the country. In whatever way it is interpreted, the word connotes the attitudes, customs and institutions that are presumed to determine—for better or for worse—the national character and face that Britain displays to the world. General talk about "the Establishment" started only in 1955. The editor of *The Establishment,* a book of vehement essays on the subject, says in his preface that in 1953 the term "was not in use at all." In more recent years it has come into use in the U.S. as well.

BRITAIN, LIFE WORLD LIBRARY

How many animal families have become extinct?

Of the 2,500 families of animals that have been discovered in the fossil record, roughly two thirds have died out without leaving descendants.

ECOLOGY, LIFE NATURE LIBRARY

F is for fish, freebooting and French-fried potatoes

Where did farming originate?

Mankind, with a two-million-year history of gathering and hunting wild foods, made the critical turn toward civilization when food crops were first cultivated around 7000 B.C. One of the first plants to be brought under cultivation was wheat, domesticated in the Middle East. Almost simultaneously, farming was invented in Central America with the domestication of vegetables like squash, and later farming arose independently in China. The secret swiftly spread to nearly every temperate, fertile part of the Old and New Worlds, and crops were swiftly diversified as men took the basic idea of cultivating plants and tried it out on the varieties that were native to each new area. By 1500 B.C. all the major food crops we now know were being grown. Today, the art of farming has been learned by every group of people on earth except the most primitive tribes, such as Australia's Warramunga aborigines.

FOOD AND NUTRITION, LIFE SCIENCE LIBRARY

What is the No. 1 farm state in the U.S.?

Agriculture is big business on the West Coast, and especially in California, which has about eight million acres of irrigated farmland, produces more than 200 crops and since 1943 has ranked as the nation's top farming state. THE PACIFIC STATES, TIME-LIFE LIBRARY OF AMERICA

How did fashion help open the American West?

High-crowned fur hats—a European status symbol for generations—were extremely popular in the United States in the early 1800s. The fur best suited for these hats was beaver, which had a unique barb that could be worked into a particularly luxuriant kind of felt. The high price paid for beaver sent a special breed of men westward into the American wilderness to search out every valley and swale where the rodent might build his dam, leading eventually to the wider exploration and settlement of the Far West. THE GROWING YEARS, THE LIFE HISTORY OF THE UNITED STATES

When does a fear become a phobia?

Everyone has fears, but fears are considered phobias only when they are so unreasonable that they interfere with normal life. Here are a few of the more than 250 things doctors have found patients to be abnormally afraid of, with the medical names for the phobias: books (bibliophobia), cats (ailurophobia), confined spaces (claustrophobia), heights (acrophobia), night (noctiphobia), ridicule (categelophobia), being stared at (ophthalmophobia), strange people (xenophobia), string (linonophobia), 13 (triskaidekaphobia), work (ergophobia) and fear (phobophobia).

THE MIND, LIFE SCIENCE LIBRARY

How many feathers has a bird?

A basic rule seems to be, not surprisingly, that the larger the bird the more numerous its feathers. A dairyman, to settle an argument, once counted all the feathers on a Plymouth Rock hen. There were 8,325. Another investigator, patiently plucking a whistling swan, amassed a record 25,216 feathers, 80 percent of which came from the head and extremely long neck. A ruby-throated hummingbird showed a low count of 940.

THE BIRDS, LIFE NATURE LIBRARY

What was the *Fianna* of ancient Ireland?

One of the most famous of ancient Irish kings was Cormac MacArt of the line of Conn, who fortified and enlarged the ancient castle on the sacred hill of Tara, near what is now Dublin, and was supported by a renowned force of warriors called the Fianna, under the command of the legendary hero Finn MacCool. To qualify for membership in the Fianna, a recruit had to memorize 12 books of poetry and run through a thick forest, leaping over branches as high as his forehead and stooping under limbs as low as his knees without snapping a twig or tearing off a leaf. He also had to be able to pull a thorn out of his foot without breaking his stride. IRELAND, LIFE WORLD LIBRARY

How do *fingernails* grow?

A man's fingernails, a ram's horns and a snail's shell share an important characteristic: all are produced by a type of growth called accretion. In human beings accretionary growth is predominantly displayed in nails, hair and bone. In these structures, living cells cast off nonliving matter, which accumulates outside the cells. The fingernail, for instance, grows from the epidermis, which secretes a soft, lifeless substance called keratin. This matter forces previously secreted keratin out from under the cuticle and forward, where it hardens and dries into a solid plate.

GROWTH, LIFE SCIENCE LIBRARY

How certain is *fingerprint* identification?

The individuality of any fingerprint has been established beyond doubt; of more than 169 million fingerprints on file with the FBI, no two are so similar that an expert cannot readily tell them apart.

THE BODY, LIFE SCIENCE LIBRARY

What were the *fireside chats?*

Franklin D. Roosevelt was the first President to recognize the potentialities of the radio for projecting his ideas and personality directly into the American home. In his fireside chats he seemed like a father talking about public affairs while sitting with his family in the living room. When Roosevelt got before a microphone, grumbled one critic, he appeared to be talking and toasting marshmallows at the same time.

NEW DEAL AND GLOBAL WAR, THE LIFE HISTORY OF THE UNITED STATES

What country catches the most fish?

Peru, with swarms of anchoveta just off its coasts, takes in more than nine million metric tons a year. Japan, long the leading fishing nation, is now second, with six million metric tons a year. There are no recent estimates available, but on the basis of old figures, Communist China undoubtedly belongs among the top three. Soviet Russia is ranked fourth, and the United States fifth. These five countries contribute well over half of the world's total. THE FISHES, LIFE NATURE LIBRARY

Is a fish always silent?

Although fish have no vocal organs, they are by no means silent. When World War II vessels with sensitive underwater listening devices reported hearing all sorts of strange beeps, grunts and groans, the Navy first thought they came from other ships. Later it was found that marine animals were responsible, that in fact the underwater world is quite a noisy place. Fish make sounds by grinding their teeth or by setting up vibrations in organs such as the swim bladder. Fishermen have since tried lowering hydrophones, but commercially valuable fish turn out to be the least loquacious, and all species tend to keep quiet near boats. THE SEA, LIFE NATURE LIBRARY

How does a fish know if it is right side up?

Most fish have small organs called statocysts, inner cavities lined with delicate hairs and containing some loose objects like a few grains of sand. Its statocysts tell a fish, even in the blackness of the abyss, whether it is right side up or upside down. THE SEA, LIFE NATURE LIBRARY

Can any fish live on land?

The clariid catfish of Africa can live for several days out of water, thanks to a treelike organ that acts as a supplement to the gills and greatly increases the surface area available for bringing oxygen into contact with the blood. This enables it to travel from one pond or river to another during dry seasons. These journeys are usually made at night by as many as 30 fish at a time, wriggling like snakes through the grass, grunting faintly as they go. How they are able to detect another water source to head for is not known. THE LAND AND WILDLIFE OF AFRICA, LIFE NATURE LIBRARY

How far can a *flea* jump?

The flea's 12-inch leap may appear modest by man's standards. But the flea actually jumps 200 times the length of its own body—the equivalent of a six-foot man bounding the length of five city blocks.

THE INSECTS, LIFE NATURE LIBRARY

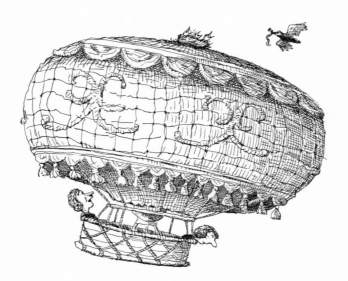

Who made the first *flight*?

On November 21, 1783, a dream as old as history became a fact. On that day two Frenchmen, Jean Pilâtre de Rozier and the Marquis d'Arlandes, flew over Paris in a balloon, traveling five and a half miles in 25 minutes. Pilâtre later attempted a more ambitious flight, but the hydrogen in his 37-foot balloon caught fire. Thus the first man to fly was also the first one to be killed in a flying accident.

MAN AND SPACE, LIFE SCIENCE LIBRARY

What is the difference between a *flounder* and a *fluke*?

Perhaps the most extraordinary change in fish shape has developed in fishes that have taken to lying on the bottom: they have become flattened. Some lie on their bellies, and these have become flattened from above; others lie on their sides and have become flattened sideways. In side-flattened fish, the flattening occurs as the young fish grows and causes a strange process in which the eyes move to the flattened—that is, upper—side of the head. Thus the flounder, which lies on its left side, has its eyes on the right side, while its close cousin the fluke, which lies on its right side, has its eyes on the left. THE FISHES, LIFE NATURE LIBRARY

How do flowers know when to bloom?

It is now known that the constantly changing relationship of daylight to darkness, as the seasons progress, determines the blossoming of flowers. This response of plants to the steadily shortening nights of spring, or to the steadily lengthening nights of fall, is known as photoperiodism. Almost every plant has a trigger that awaits the proper photoperiodic signal that tells its cells to stop growing stems and leaves and start growing flowers and seeds. THE FOREST, LIFE NATURE LIBRARY

Can man ever fly under his own power?

A human being is simply not designed to fly. He is heavy and unstreamlined, and his bone structure and muscle arrangement are completely unsuited to handling wings. A man weighing 150 pounds would have to have a breastbone protruding six feet in order to accommodate the muscles needed to power a set of wings capable of lifting him off the ground. FLIGHT, LIFE SCIENCE LIBRARY

What foods do we owe to the Indians?

Ancient Indian plant breeders of Middle and South America domesticated many plants that now play a vital role in feeding the world. Corn is a primary food in most countries that are not too cold and sunless for its cultivation. White potatoes developed by the highland Indians of Peru have become a firmly established staple in lands with coolish climates. Sweet potatoes of the South American tropical forest are equally important in warm countries. Kidney beans (Mexican) are the poor man's source of protein nearly everywhere except the Far East. And peanuts (Peruvian) are an essential part of the diet in large parts of Africa. The long list also includes lima beans, tomatoes, peppers, most kinds of squash and pumpkins, avocados, cocoa, pineapples and many lesser crops.

ANCIENT AMERICA, GREAT AGES OF MAN

What causes freckles?

Except in the case of albinos, every person's skin has cells called melanocytes, which produce a certain amount of melanin, a dark pigment
that absorbs ultraviolet light. These cells produce melanin at increasing
rates when the skin is exposed to sunlight—hence the sunbather's tan.
Some melanocytes are more active than others. Thus when groups of active melanocytes are surrounded by groups of less active melanocytes,
the results are islands of pigment known as freckles. THE BODY, LIFE SCIENCE LIBRARY

What was freebooting?

Freebooting was the eminently practical process of letting the Spanish ex-
plorers find booty and then taking it away from them. It was passably
profitable for a number of years, but it took a resourceful freebooter
named Giovanni da Verrazano, the discoverer of New York Harbor, to
widen the eyes of the business community. He saw his chance in 1523
and cut out from the Spanish fleet two of the ships carrying home part
of the vast treasure the conquistador Hernán Cortés had seized from the
coffers of Moctezuma, the Aztec ruler of Mexico. The loot was fab-
ulous: gold, emeralds, pumas, cloaks and pearls; the weight of the pearls
alone came to 680 pounds. THE WEST INDIES, LIFE WORLD LIBRARY

Where were French-fried potatoes invented?

The prospect of dinner does not stay the Belgians from pausing for a
snack in the streets. This treat is usually a paper cone of French-fried
potatoes—which the Belgians (not the French) invented. The Belgians
call them *patates frites* and buy them at corner stands, from which
emanates the pervasive national odor: hot vegetable oil.

THE LOW COUNTRIES, LIFE WORLD LIBRARY

How does the frigate bird feed?

The frigate bird is a superb flier, as well as an unmitigated pirate. In feeding, it hovers gracefully above other birds, waits for one to catch a fish,
then sweeps unerringly to the attack, forcing the victim to drop its prize.
The frigate bird then snatches the falling fish in mid-air, gulps it down
and climbs aloft to wait for another morsel. EVOLUTION, LIFE NATURE LIBRARY

What do *frogs* have in common with crocodiles and hippopotamuses?

Frogs are amphibians, crocodiles are reptiles, and hippopotamuses are mammals—but all three breathe air and live in water. Hence they all have nostrils and eyes that protrude above the surface when their bodies are submerged—an example of convergent evolution.

ECOLOGY, LIFE NATURE LIBRARY

Does *frost* paint the leaves in autumn?

Tranquil autumn beauty stems from a chemical reaction, repeated a millionfold in turning leaves, in which pigments and weather play an equal role. As the season of leaf activity ends, production of chlorophyll, whose green pigment has predominated throughout the spring and summer, wanes and the yellow carotenoids at last reveal themselves, particularly in elms, birches and poplars. In oaks and maples, anthocyanins form when sugar is trapped in the leaves by sudden cold snaps, and the trees flaunt their brilliant reds. This yearly display is usually most spectacular in New England, where early frosts are commonly followed by warm spells, and deciduous trees are abundant. THE PLANTS, LIFE NATURE LIBRARY

G is for General Motors, ginkgo trees and gypsies

Who carried the message to *Garcia*?

Because Army Lieutenant Andres S. Rowan had written a good book about Cuba, he was given the risky job of delivering a message behind Spanish lines to the insurgent Cuban General Calixto Garcia during the Spanish-American War. Not till well after the fact did anyone realize that author Rowan had never before been to Cuba.

REACHING FOR EMPIRE, THE LIFE HISTORY OF THE UNITED STATES

Who founded *General Motors*?

William Crapo Durant, a well-to-do carriage maker in Flint, Michigan, took over the young, undercapitalized Buick company in 1904. With this as a start, and at a time when the automobile was still a novelty, Durant began to construct the concept of a great combination of auto companies. By 1910 he had brought together 12 auto producers, including

Oldsmobile, Oakland (later Pontiac) and Cadillac, as the General Motors Company. When he tried to buy out Henry Ford, the story goes, Ford was willing but demanded payment of eight million dollars in cash. Durant had no such liquid reserve, and the deal fell through.

WAR, BOOM AND BUST, THE LIFE HISTORY OF THE UNITED STATES

Why are **ginkgo trees** common in cities?

Ginkgos date back to the age of the dinosaur and once grew wild over much of the earth, including Greenland, but only a single species survives today. It was discovered in China by European travelers about 250 years ago and has since been widely planted as an ornamental tree throughout much of the range where it once flourished wild. The ginkgo, or maidenhair tree, is often seen in North American cities, for this hardy survivor is one of the few trees in the world that can endure the poisonous soot of the modern metropolis. Its fanlike, veined leaves are unlike those of any other existing plants. THE FOREST, LIFE NATURE LIBRARY

How much faster do **girls** mature than boys?

X-rays of both hand and knee show that girls are on the average about 20 per cent ahead of boys at any age up to physical maturity. Until the age of five months, girls lead in the ability to perform the movements that are prerequisite for creeping, sitting and walking, and even after that they generally remain ahead in acquiring skills that demand fine movements and motor coordination, such as tying bows or skipping. But no evidence of brain difference between the sexes has yet emerged.

GROWTH, LIFE SCIENCE LIBRARY

Why do **glaciers** flow?

Glaciers, colossal masses of ice capable of grinding up mountains, form where freezing temperatures permit the packing-down of the snows of many years. In Greenland, 10,000 centuries of snow have formed an ice-cap 10,000 feet high. Under so much snow, internal pressure may reach seven tons to the square foot. The bottom layers of ice become so compressed that they start slipping and begin to flow in much the same fashion as a river, although the glacier may take centuries to creep down a mountain valley. WATER, LIFE SCIENCE LIBRARY

Do glaciers exist in the Torrid Zone?

Africa's Mount Kenya (17,040 feet) boasts several glaciers, even though it straddles the equator—a fact that offers the interesting possibility that a person could get frostbite while standing on the equator, or for that matter freeze to death.   TROPICAL AFRICA, LIFE WORLD LIBRARY

Why do the gods of ancient Rome parallel those of Greece?

The Romans became so influenced by Greek culture that they blended the Greek gods into their own pantheon. Thus the West sometimes knows Zeus as Jupiter or Jove, Poseidon as Neptune, and Hades as Pluto. Athena is the Roman Minerva, Aphrodite is Venus, and Hermes is Mercury. Artemis became Diana, and Dionysus, Bacchus.

GREECE, LIFE WORLD LIBRARY

What is the Golden Ratio in art and architecture?

The so-called Golden Ratio, or Golden Section, which has intrigued experts in mathematics and esthetics for centuries, derives from the number sequence discovered by the medieval Italian mathematician Leopold ("Fibonacci") da Pisa. The Fibonacci series starts with 1 and adds the last two numbers to arrive at the next: 1, 1, 2, 3, 5, 8, 13, 21, 34, etc. The ratio between any two adjacent Fibonacci numbers after 3 is $1:1.618$. This ratio occurs notably in the Golden Rectangle, a figure whose two sides bear the magic relationship to each other. The Golden Rectangle is said to be one of the most visually satisfying of all geometric forms; for years experts have been finding examples of it in art masterpieces dating back to the edifices of ancient Greece.   MATHEMATICS, LIFE SCIENCE LIBRARY

How fierce are gorillas?

Despite all the atrocities falsely attributed to them, gorillas are essentially peace-loving creatures that would rather retreat than fight, except in circumstances when their lives are threatened and retreat is impossible. In the wild they have never been seen eating meat, although individuals have learned to do so in captivity. Their gentle nature is evident at an early age: at play, juvenile gorillas are markedly solicitous of often-turbulent infants.   THE PRIMATES, LIFE NATURE LIBRARY

How extensive are **grass roots?**

A single rye plant, after four months of growth, was found to have put out 378 miles of roots, or an average of three miles in a single day. This growth was accomplished by 14 million separate roots having a total of about 14 billion root hairs. THE FOREST, LIFE NATURE LIBRARY

Did Newton discover **gravity?**

Sir Isaac Newton did not discover gravitation by watching an apple fall or by being hit by one, as in popular legend. Laws relating to falling objects had been studied extensively, but they had been applied only on the surface of the earth. There was no idea of gravitation as a universal force that affects all objects wherever they may be. Obviously, said the reasoning of the time, it does not apply to the heavenly bodies, since they do not fall to the earth. Newton showed his genius by applying the laws of falling bodies to the unfalling moon. PLANETS, LIFE SCIENCE LIBRARY

How old is the **Great Wall of China?**

It came into being in the Third Century B.C. when the Emperor Shih Huang Ti joined and extended walls previously built by feudal warriors. Some 1,500 miles in length, the Great Wall provided protection against invaders. Behind it the Chinese developed a civilization unmatched by any of the peoples on their borders. With distance, topography and the sea continuing to isolate them from peoples whose societies were comparable to their own, the Chinese came to feel more and more superior to outsiders as the centuries advanced. CHINA, LIFE WORLD LIBRARY

Do **growth** patterns of childhood predict final height?

Speed of growth is not decisive in fixing a child's final height. True, some slow-growing children never become tall. But others, simply by continuing to grow for a longer time, may end up above average height. GROWTH, LIFE SCIENCE LIBRARY

Does human **growth** stop after adolescence?

Growth may continue, although slowly, for many years after adolescence. Some people are still growing—though almost imperceptibly—in their forties. For all practical purposes, however, growth ceases in the teens. On the average, boys reach 98 per cent of their final height by the time they are 17¾, girls by the time they are 16½. GROWTH, LIFE SCIENCE LIBRARY

Who are the true **gypsies?**

Strictly speaking, gypsies are members of groups that are believed to have migrated from India to Europe about 1000 A.D. They speak a language called Romany, which is derived from Sanskrit. IRELAND, LIFE WORLD LIBRARY

H is for hippopotamuses, Ho Chi Minh and hypnosis

How many people in the U.S. are hard of hearing?

Defective hearing is the most common physical impairment in the U.S. One out of every 20 Americans has some degree of hearing loss. Over 300,000 are so deaf that they cannot hear human speech, no matter how strongly amplified. SOUND AND HEARING, LIFE SCIENCE LIBRARY

How large is the human heart?

The heart is no bigger than a good-sized fist. It weighs less than a pound, and its shape resembles the popular Valentine image sufficiently to satisfy the sentimentalists. Divided down the middle by a partition of muscle, it is like two pumps back to back, with valve-controlled openings at the top and bottom of each side. To get from one side to the other, the blood must go the long way around, through the body.

THE BODY, LIFE SCIENCE LIBRARY

Is human height increasing?

The past several centuries have witnessed pronounced increases in the
height of populations all around the world. For example, most modern
soldiers would have a hard time fitting into medieval armor. Houses
built in New England 300 years ago seem quaint today because of the di-
minutive size of everything, particularly the height of doorways. Scientists
still have not pinpointed the exact cause of this accelerated growth. Environmental changes such as improvements in public health, nutrition
and child care are unquestionably responsible to some degree, but there
seem to be genetic factors at work too.　　　　GROWTH. LIFE SCIENCE LIBRARY

Which animals really hibernate?

Many mammals retire to their underground burrows in the fall or early
winter and sleep through the cold months. Bears, skunks and possums,
among others, lapse into prolonged but fairly normal slumber, for they
wake up from time to time and move about. But others—woodchucks,
jumping mice and ground squirrels, for example—are true hibernators.
When a ground squirrel hibernates, its body temperature sometimes

drops to only a few degrees above freezing. From a normal 200 to 400 beats per minute its heart may slow to five, and its breathing from nearly 200 respirations per minute to four or less. Hibernating woodchucks have been observed breathing only once every five minutes.

THE MAMMALS, LIFE NATURE LIBRARY

Is *Hinduism* a religion?

Hinduism is generally described as a religion, but it is far more than that. And if religion is thought of in the Western sense as confined to creed and worship, the description is misleading. Hinduism is a complete rule of life, and every act in the orthodox Hindu's existence—rising in the morning, bathing, eating, praying, even the sex act—is regulated by rituals. The rules of Hinduism may be interpreted one way in one community and quite a different way in another. At its highest level it is a lofty speculative philosophy, mystic and monotheistic, which enjoins an ascetic rejection of the world of the flesh because it considers man's span on earth to be merely a passing moment in the soul's long journey through time.

INDIA, LIFE WORLD LIBRARY

What does a *hippopotamus* eat?

The cavernous mouths and ponderous tusks of the hippopotamus suggest that it feeds by uprooting aquatic plants or that it chomps up great volumes of floating vegetation. This is not the case. Hippopotamuses are efficient and inveterate grazers. At night all the hippos go ashore and push their vast muzzles into the turf, and clip grass as neatly as a sheep. They eat 50 or more pounds dry weight of grass during a night.

THE LAND AND WILDLIFE OF AFRICA, LIFE NATURE LIBRARY

What European country is a major exporter of *hippopotamuses?*

The 123 thermal springs of Budapest, Hungary, contain sulfur, carbonic acid, lime, calcium and salt, as well as other substances. Among the possible beneficiaries have been the hippopotamuses at the city zoo. They wallowed in these mineral waters after their arrival at the zoo a number of years ago and began breeding vigorously, an unprecedented event in zoological history. Hungary has since been blessed with a valuable export: baby hippos.

EASTERN EUROPE, LIFE WORLD LIBRARY

How did **Ho Chi Minh** become a Communist?

A vast variety of nationalist movements and individuals sprouted in Vietnam between the two World Wars, and out of all this ferment came a single strong individual who was an equally firm Communist. His real name is still unknown, but the most famous of his many aliases is Ho Chi Minh —"He who enlightens." When the Paris Peace Conference convened in 1919, Ho sent the leaders of the victorious Allied powers a memorandum calling for the application of President Wilson's principles of self-determination of peoples to Vietnam. The document was, of course, disregarded. Within a year Ho was a member of the newly organized French Communist Party.   SOUTHEAST ASIA, LIFE WORLD LIBRARY

Why is the Netherlands sometimes called **Holland**?

Since the 16th Century, the official name of the Dutch homeland has been the Netherlands, but Dutchmen have given up trying to bring this to the attention of foreigners, who persist in calling the country Holland. The use of the term is, however, widely accepted. For centuries practically everyone who arrived on foreign shores from the Netherlands area was a "Hollander"—a native of the province of Holland. To this day Holland remains the Netherlands' most important region.

THE LOW COUNTRIES, LIFE WORLD LIBRARY

Is the **horse** native to North America?

There are several species of mammals that originated in North America, walked across land now under the Bering Strait into Asia—and then became extinct here. The horse is one: it died out in North America as a native animal perhaps 10,000 years ago and did not reappear here until the Spanish conquistadors brought horses to Mexico in the 16th Century. The wild mustangs of the American West were the descendants of those Spanish imports.   ECOLOGY, LIFE NATURE LIBRARY

Does the **Hudson Bay Company** still trade furs?

The Bay has moved with the times; while it still maintains two outposts and 28 other stores, many above the Arctic Circle, its Northern operations account for a tiny fraction of its gross income. Its trading posts in the Prairies have blossomed into big department stores, and it now is Canada's third largest retailer, sells its own brand of Scotch whiskey and has moved into the oil business. But the Bay is still the Bay; in remote arctic outposts, Bay managers are still called on to settle Eskimo family quarrels and dole out family allowance money, and it continues its traditional trade with fur trappers. CANADA, LIFE WORLD LIBRARY

Is hypnosis dangerous?

Ever since its formal introduction in the 18th Century, hypnosis has been the subject of argument on ethical grounds: most people find the idea that one person can be made completely subject to the will of another intrinsically alarming. But hypnosis requires a relationship of trust between the hypnotist and his subject; it is improbable that anyone can be hypnotized against his will. And even a subject in deep hypnotic trance is not likely to be persuaded to violate his own moral code, for although hypnosis can bring certain behavior patterns to the surface, it cannot create new patterns that are foreign to the subject's personality.

THE MIND, LIFE SCIENCE LIBRARY

I is for identical humans, I.Q. and Italian women

Can *identical humans* be born?

The odds against two individuals being born exactly alike are astronomical (except for identical twins, who both come from one fertilized egg and do indeed have the same assortment of genes). There are more than eight million ways the 23 chromosomes of a human mother and the 23 of a father can combine. The odds against any two of their children having the same complement of chromosomes are about 70 trillion to 1. And since each chromosome may have 1,250 genes, the odds against two identical individuals reach a number so high, it doesn't even have a name; it would have to be written as 1 followed by 9,031 zeros.   THE CELL, LIFE SCIENCE LIBRARY

What are the languages of *India?*

Altogether some 845 languages and dialects are spoken. Most of these are used by relatively small numbers of people, and the Indian constitution gives official status to only 14 of them. Theoretically, English is scheduled to lose its position as an official medium of communication, but most educated Indians speak it, the top government officials use it, and most of the proceedings in Parliament and in the Supreme Court are in it. Hindi was recently chosen as India's national tongue—but is unknown to millions.   INDIA, LIFE WORLD LIBRARY

Why does the music of *India* sound so exotic?

Except for the popular or "film" music that Indians have borrowed from the West, classical Indian music is marked by a total absence of harmony, relying solely on melody for its effect. The heart of classical Indian music is a melodic form known as the *raga*. Some 70,000 *ragas* exist, but very few musicians have mastered all of them. The musician is given some liberty for improvisation as he performs a *raga*, but must not deviate either from the rhythm or from the basic mood and melodic framework.   INDIA, LIFE WORLD LIBRARY

What conquered the American *Indian*?

Television and movie epics to the contrary, it was not the pioneer who subdued the Indians but rather smallpox. European settlers in North America soon became aware that smallpox was one of the best weapons against the Indians, and they even intentionally spread the disease by means of infected blankets.   ECOLOGY, LIFE NATURE LIBRARY

What was the greatest *Indian* city of the Americas?

Tenochtitlan (now Mexico City) was settled about 1325. By 1519, the year of the Spanish invasion, it had become a city of great size and magnificence, about five times as large as the London of that time. Most of the oval island on which Tenochtitlan stood was swampland that was filled with silt dredged from the lake bottom and with earth brought from the mainland in canoes. The city was connected to the mainland by three long causeways. The meaner houses were made of adobe, the better ones of stone and stucco, but all were cleanly whitewashed. Most of them had courtyards, some of which resembled small parks, and everywhere bloomed flowers, which the fierce Aztecs loved inordinately.   ANCIENT AMERICA, GREAT AGES OF MAN

How strong is an *insect*?

Insects seem endowed with physical strength out of all proportion to their size. An ant can pick up a stone some 50 times its own weight. But by putting small loads on wheels so they can be pulled, experimenters have found that a bee can haul a burden 300 times its own weight—which is roughly equivalent to a human pulling three 10-ton trailer trucks at the same time. THE INSECTS, LIFE NATURE LIBRARY

How long can an *insect* live without a head?

Each of an insect's three body divisions is semiautonomous and can carry out reflex actions on its own without first having to go through the switchboard of the brain. Even when an insect is decapitated it may continue to react automatically to light, temperature, humidity, chemicals and various other stimuli. A headless insect may live for as much as a year, until it starves to death. The cutoff abdomen of a moth is capable of being fertilized and laying eggs. THE INSECTS, LIFE NATURE LIBRARY

What is the life expectancy of *insects*?

Some insect species have brief spans of life: one kind of aphid can become adult in as little as six days, spend the next four or five days in reproduction, and then die. At the other end of the scale, there are some insects that are enormously long-lived: queen termites may survive for more than 50 years. THE INSECTS, LIFE NATURE LIBRARY

Can environment affect *I.Q.?*

It is generally agreed that intelligence is related to the number and nature of the interconnections among the cells of the brain, and to the action of the various chemical substances it secretes. The development of intelligence, precocious or otherwise, is much influenced by the child's environment. Indeed, environmental changes are presumed responsible for an apparent rise in the general level of intelligence—at least as measured by I.Q. tests—among American children. GROWTH, LIFE SCIENCE LIBRARY

How large is *Israel?*

Not counting occupied regions, the country is only one quarter the size of Maine and covers an area of 8,000 square miles—only one quarter of 1 per cent of that occupied by its Arab neighbors. If all the adult Israelis were to stand in a single line on their country's 750-mile perimeter, they would just about be able to touch fingers. ISRAEL, LIFE WORLD LIBRARY

How emancipated are the women of *Italy?*

It is only in the progressive and prosperous cities of northern Italy and in Rome that a young woman is permitted to go out alone with a young man. As one moves from north to south, customs alter. In Milan, a young girl can live away from home, hold a responsible job, and come and go as she pleases. In Rome, however, a girl under 35 living separately from her parents is something of a rarity. And although change is stirring the scene, the South still holds largely to the mores of a century ago, as illustrated recently when a 25-year-old Sicilian girl judged herself so irreparably damaged by having received a kiss that she shot the transgressor when he refused to marry her. ITALY, LIFE WORLD LIBRARY

What country sends the most tourists to *Italy?*

Germans are the largest group of visitors; after them are the Austrians, Swiss, French and British. Americans rank only sixth, though they stay longer and spend more. ITALY, LIFE WORLD LIBRARY

73

J is for Japan, jet flights and Jews

What does the name Japan mean?

The Japanese derive the name of their country from a Chinese phrase meaning "the source of the sun." The phrase describes the country's geographical position east of China. The word "Japan" came from Marco Polo's attempt to render the Chinese pronunciation of the phrase in Italian after his return from China in the 13th Century. The Japanese themselves, however, usually give the characters a sound that is rendered in English as "Nihon."

JAPAN, LIFE WORLD LIBRARY

How long has one family ruled Japan?

The same family—originally the principal clan in the Kyoto-Osaka area—has occupied the Japanese throne since the Sixth Century A.D., when Buddhism was imported from Korea. Hirohito is the 124th holder of the title.

JAPAN, LIFE WORLD LIBRARY

What are the origins of jazz?

Jazz sprang from many sources, among them spirituals, old ballads, children's jingles, minstrel music, the ragtime piano of red-light districts—and funeral processions. An old man who lived in New Orleans once recalled how it was: "On the way out to the cemetery, before they bury the man, the band played most all hymns, like 'Just a Closer Walk with Thee.' But once they left there, then they started to swing. They wouldn't be 25 feet from the graveyard before they hit 'Didn't He Ramble.' . . . Then they'd play 'Sing On' or 'The Saints.' . . . Finally the band would get to the lodge hall and break up and that was always the end of a perfect death." WAR, BOOM AND BUST, THE LIFE HISTORY OF THE UNITED STATES

What gives *"The Jazz Singer"* a special place in film history?

It was the first feature film with synchronized music and dialogue, appearing in 1927 and starring Al Jolson. At the time movie producers considered sound a passing fad. But by 1929 silent movies were rapidly vanishing, and theater attendance had almost doubled—to 5.7 billion a year. WAR, BOOM AND BUST, THE LIFE HISTORY OF THE UNITED STATES

Why is *Jerusalem* such a focal point of reverence and contention?

Down through the ages this ancient capital city has meant more to more people than any other human dwelling place. The rocky approaches to the city have been stained with the blood of millions of men who fought in the name of a religion or of nationalism, or merely because of some tyrant's lust for power. Canaanites, Amorites, Egyptians, Babylonians, Persians, Greeks, Syrians, Romans, Crusaders, Saracens, Frenchmen, Germans, Austrians, Turks, the British, all at one time or another fought over what Jews, Christians and Moslems alike today call the Holy City—because it is in Jerusalem that David and Solomon ruled, Jesus taught and suffered, and Mohammed is believed to have ascended to heaven. ISRAEL, LIFE WORLD LIBRARY

How does a *jet engine* work?

The turbojet engine derives its name from the turbine—a bladed wheel that functions like a small, multiwinged windmill—placed at the back of the combustion chamber. The engine has no propeller. It is called a "reaction" engine because, as it shoots a continuous blast of hot gases rearward, it reacts by moving forward itself. The effect is the same as when a child inflates a toy balloon, holds its stem, then lets go; air rushing out of the stem propels the balloon through the air.

When did the first jet flight take place?

In 1935 a German physics student named Hans von Ohain patented an engine design. Within a year the Heinkel aircraft company had hired Von Ohain to develop his engine, and by March 1937 he had built a small, 550-pound-thrust demonstration model of the power plant that led impressed Heinkel officials to order construction of a flight version. The first Von Ohain engine, designed for about 1,850 pounds thrust, fell far short of its rating. Heinkel and Von Ohain then developed a modified version of 1,100 pounds thrust that met all expectations. The engine was installed in a Heinkel He 178 fighter, and history's first turbojet flight took place on August 27, 1939, five days before Hitler's armies invaded Poland.

What proportion of the world's Jews live in Israel?

After more than a decade of intensive immigration, only about 16 per cent of world Jewry live in Israel. The successful ingathering of more than one million Jews has not decreased the interest of government leaders in further immigration. There are more than 12 million Jews in the world outside Israel, including 5.5 million in the United States, 500,000 in France and 450,000 in Great Britain. Only a few thousand from these countries have settled in Israel, because most are content in their own lands. And in countries where there is more discrimination or persecution, it is impossible to leave. The greatest number of potential immigrants—an estimated three million—live in Russia, but permission to leave for Israel is denied them. ISRAEL, LIFE WORLD LIBRARY

What is the unit of measurement known as the jnd?

The initials stand for the "just noticeable difference" between sensations. Researchers ask an experimental subject to judge between two stimuli— two sounds of nearly identical intensity, two lights of similar brightness or color, two weights that are nearly the same. By repeated tests, an effort is made to establish the exact difference between stimuli that is needed to produce a single jnd of sensation. SOUND AND HEARING, LIFE SCIENCE LIBRARY

K is for kangaroos, Captain Kidd and koalas

*How far can a **kangaroo** jump?*

One large kangaroo, at a single desperate bound, is reported to have cleared a pile of timber 10½ feet high and 27 feet long.

THE LAND AND WILDLIFE OF AUSTRALIA, LIFE NATURE LIBRARY

*Whatever happened to **Captain Kidd?***

The American colonists were of two minds about piracy. Though they passed laws that punished piracy with death, they welcomed freebooters to their ports because they came to replenish supplies and paid in needed silver and gold coin. As piracy increased, Parliament also made the crime a capital offense. Under the act of 1699, a New York sea captain of Scottish origin named Captain William Kidd was convicted in London and hanged at Wapping. The legend lives on that he successfully buried most of his treasure, and romantics have been searching the highlands of the lower Hudson River and dredging the coves and inlets of Long Island ever since in futile efforts to find the loot.

THE NEW WORLD, THE LIFE HISTORY OF THE UNITED STATES

Is the **koala** a fussy eater?

Apparently the cuddlesome, Teddy-bearish koala has been shaped by one of the most extreme specializations of plant eating ever developed in a mammal. Woolly, snub-nosed, round-eared, about 30 pounds in weight and about two and a half feet long when fully grown, the koala lives exclusively on eucalyptus leaves—and more specifically on those of some 12 smooth-barked species, only a few of which are really preferred. To most other animals, these leaves are oily and poisonous. An adult koala consumes some two and a half pounds of these leaves a night—and nothing else. Indeed, the name koala is an aboriginal one meaning "no drink."

THE LAND AND WILDLIFE OF AUSTRALIA, LIFE NATURE LIBRARY

How American was the **Korean War?**

Since the United States provided a disproportionate share of the troops, the United Nations intervention seemed to most Americans to be simply a United States engagement. In the end, the United States supplied roughly 33 per cent of the U.N. forces; the Republic of Korea, 61 per cent; other nations, less than 6 per cent.

THE GREAT AGE OF CHANGE, THE LIFE HISTORY OF THE UNITED STATES

L is for land tides, life expectancy and llamas

What are land tides?

The moon has captured the imagination of man. But it also exerts a strong physical influence on the earth. It is so close (only about 240,000 miles away) that its gravitational pull is powerfully felt. The oceans are heaped into tides and even the land is affected. The North American continent may rise as much as six inches when the moon is overhead.

THE EARTH, LIFE NATURE LIBRARY

How similar are the languages of Spain and Portugal?

Like French, Italian and Romanian, the two languages have evolved from dialects of Latin. Neither one is an offshoot of the other. Like brothers, they have a common parentage, but they have gone their separate ways for so long that a speaker of Spanish would not understand Portuguese if he were hearing it for the first time.

BRAZIL, LIFE WORLD LIBRARY

*How did the **Latin Quarter** of Paris get its name?*

On the left bank of the Seine in Paris is a low hill whose slopes have been known for centuries as the Latin Quarter. Here in the Middle Ages students debated all kinds of questions in Latin, hence the name. Here grew up a famous university, the University of Paris, whose liberal arts college is now called the Sorbonne. France, Life World Library

*Does **life** exist on other planets?*

Despite its 10-billion-mile diameter, the solar system, presided over by the sun, is dwarfed by the Milky Way, to which it belongs. But the Milky Way itself, containing 100 billion stars, is only a mote in the universe. There are billions of such galaxies, each with its own myriad stars, and most of these stars have their own planetary systems. If only 1/10,000 of 1 per cent of those planets harbor a technical civilization—and this seems to be a conservative estimate—the universe must teem with more than 100 trillion civilizations. Planets, Life Science Library

*When is **life** likely to end on earth?*

Not for at least three billion years—perhaps not for 10 billion years, or about twice as long as the earth and solar system have existed up to now. Astronomers predict that then the sun will pass through a "red giant" stage before turning into a cold, dark lump of matter drifting through space. When the sun turns into a red giant, it will swell to nearly 100 times its present size, emitting immense quantities of heat in the process. In its baleful red light the earth's temperature will rise inexorably. Life will shrivel and the seas will boil away in clouds of steam. Some of the steam will escape into space, but the bulk of it will fall back to earth when the sun cools again. As the solar furnace burns lower and lower, what is left of the oceans will slowly freeze. In time they will become solid ice, and in this form they will endure as long as the earth endures. The Sea, Life Nature Library

*What is the **life expectancy** of animals?*

Although man has increased the life expectancy of his kind by controlling many natural hazards, he has not been able to prevent aging. Among all warm-blooded animals a potentially longer life is linked to large size, low reproductive rate and slow maturing. Many cold-blooded ones, by contrast, may have no fixed adult size and grow until they die—as most wild animals do—of predation or disease. Theoretically, such an animal, if completely protected, should never die at all. ECOLOGY, LIFE NATURE LIBRARY

*Where is human **life expectancy** the greatest?*

In prosperous Sweden poverty is virtually unknown, and the best medical care is available to all. The healthiest people in this healthy land are those of the professional class, who may have the best health record in the world. These people are cared for, quite literally, from birth until death, sheltered in clean houses, treated in the most up-to-date hospitals. As a result, the average life expectancy in Sweden is the world's highest—71.6 years for men, 75.4 for women. HEALTH AND DISEASE, LIFE SCIENCE LIBRARY

*Is there a limit to man's potential **life span**?*

Modern medicine has lengthened the probable life span of the human organism. In this century there has been a notable increase in the number of people living into their seventh, eighth or even ninth decade. Interestingly, there has not been a proportionate increase in the number of centenarians. This suggests that there may be a species-wide, genetically determined limit to the life expectancy of both cells and the organism they constitute. THE CELL, LIFE SCIENCE LIBRARY

*Who won the **Lincoln-Douglas debates**?*

Stephen A. Douglas narrowly won re-election to the Senate, but he was no longer the unquestioned leader of his party or the idol of the North. Abraham Lincoln, a new and towering figure who would loom ever larger, had been projected onto the political scene.

THE UNION SUNDERED, THE LIFE HISTORY OF THE UNITED STATES

*Can **liquor** warm you up?*

In the circulatory system, alcohol causes the capillaries that are located just under the skin to dilate so they can carry more blood. The skin, flushed with warm blood, feels warmer. So does the drinker—but this, like many effects of alcohol, is an illusion. In fact, body temperature does not rise but falls, because much internal heat is carried by blood to the skin and dissipated there. Despite the folklore of the St. Bernard dog that brought comfort with its keg of brandy to travelers marooned in snowdrifts, alcohol has never kept anyone warm in cold weather. Indeed, in really cold weather it can lead to dangerous chilling.

DRUGS, LIFE SCIENCE LIBRARY

Of what use is the *llama*?

Although it is slow and contrary and will carry no more than 100 pounds, the llama of the Andes is used as a beast of burden. It provides wool and is a source of tallow, leather and meat. Its droppings are gathered for fuel. The llama is even used for sacrifice and soothsaying. It is suspicious of all strange humans, particularly white ones, and it may spit, bite or kick. Or it may lie down with its load and groan.

THE ANDEAN REPUBLICS, LIFE WORLD LIBRARY

How bad is a *locust plague*?

"Locust" is the common name for several species of short-horned grasshoppers that often increase suddenly in numbers and undertake mass migrations. There are seven or so species that can bring desolation and famine in their wake. One such locust swarm in East Africa was over a hundred feet deep on a mile-wide front: it took nine hours to pass at a speed of about six miles an hour.

THE INSECTS, LIFE NATURE LIBRARY

M is for mavericks, missing-link fossils and movie stars

*How modern is **make-up**?*

The scope of human vanity is far from a new story. In 1770 an Eng-
lishman who may have been soured by personal experience introduced
into Parliament a bill that revealed the wide range of surface attractions
employed by women of the realm. He proposed to pin a witchcraft
charge on any of them—"of whatever age, rank, profession, or degree,
whether virgins, maids, or widows"—who lured one of His Majesty's
subjects into matrimony by the use of "scents, paints, cosmetic washes,
artificial teeth, false hair, Spanish wool, iron stays, hoops, high heeled
shoes, bolstered hips." If he had bothered to check his history, he
would have known that he was fighting a losing battle. Far earlier, as
evidenced by artifacts from ancient Egypt, a wealthy Egyptian woman
was likely to have a full supply of pots for holding kohl (an eye shadow still used today), sticks for applying kohl, hair tweezers, combs,
curlers and mirrors.   THE BODY, LIFE SCIENCE LIBRARY; ANCIENT EGYPT, GREAT AGES OF MAN

What is the oldest **manufacturing company** in the world still functioning today?

Sweden's Stora Kopparbergs Bergslags Aktiebolag, whose wealth rests on the two complementary assets of ore and timber, dates back to the 13th Century.

SCANDINAVIA, LIFE WORLD LIBRARY

What was the childhood religion of **Mao Tse-tung?**

In his early youth Mao, the high priest of Chinese Communism, was a devout Buddhist, and he also used to quote the Confucian classics in arguments with his domineering father. Even after he had abandoned Buddhism and begun to toy with Marxism at Peking University, Mao occasionally visited the neighboring province of Shantung to view Confucius' grave and the birthplace of Mencius, Confucius' disciple.

CHINA, LIFE WORLD LIBRARY

What was **marriage** like in ancient Mexico?

When the young people of a community reached marriageable age—about 20 for boys, 16 for girls—they were lined up in two rows facing each other and an official declared them engaged. This was not really the act of cold-hearted tyranny that it seems. The boys and girls had already paired off; the official's main function was to settle disputes between rivals for a girl and to give the Emperor's blessing to the unions. Later the marriage ceremonies were performed according to local custom.

ANCIENT AMERICA, GREAT AGES OF MAN

Does life exist on **Mars?**

Persistent speculation that there may be intelligent beings on Mars reached extravagant proportions early in the 20th Century after American astronomer Percival Lowell interpreted the markings on Mars, seen by several astronomers, as canals that were the product of a culture far in advance of the earth's. Today, most astronomers believe that canals do not exist on Mars, at least in the form depicted by Lowell. Nevertheless, most think that there may be some life forms on the red planet. They point to a change on Mars in spring, when the surface shades turn darker, as a phenomenon that may be evidence of life. PLANETS, LIFE SCIENCE LIBRARY

Where was "The Marseillaise" composed?

The French national anthem, the most famous patriotic song in the world, was written in the mercantile Alsatian city of Strasbourg in northeastern France. It got its name from the fiery militiamen of Marseilles, who sang it while marching north to Paris on their way to dethrone King Louis XVI in 1792. FRANCE, LIFE WORLD LIBRARY

Why did the actors of ancient Greece wear masks?

Greek theaters were so large that it was hard to communicate moods and feelings to distant spectators. To help overcome this, actors wore thick-soled boots and robes with sleeves, creating a larger-than-life appearance. But the device most used to reach the audience was masks. The masks instantly identified a character as old or young, man or woman, happy or sad. They were often made with calm expressions on one side and angry ones on the other, enabling the actor to change moods with one swift movement of his head. And in addition to these visual effects, they had funnel-shaped mouths that acted as megaphones to project the voice. CLASSICAL GREECE, GREAT AGES OF MAN

Who was the first maverick?

In the early days of the open range in Texas, a yearling calf belonged to any man who could rope and brand it. Soon, to protect the four-footed property, 5,000 brands—initials, numerals and emblems—were registered. Samuel Maverick, who refused to brand his calves, lost a lot of cattle but gave his name to the language as a synonym for a nonconformist. THE AGE OF STEEL AND STEAM, THE LIFE HISTORY OF THE UNITED STATES

Why do so many U.S. merchant ships fly foreign flags?

For shipowners, the practice is advantageous. The tax rates on such vessels are lower than on U.S.-registered ships, and they may pay crewmen of other than U.S. nationality the wage rates of their own countries, which average 70 to 80 per cent less than American union scales. The practice is known as flying the "flag of convenience" or the "flag of necessity." Some 450 vessels, one half of the U.S. Merchant Marine, fly foreign flags. CENTRAL AMERICA, LIFE WORLD LIBRARY

What stand did Lincoln take on the **Mexican War?**

Abraham Lincoln fought against the war in Congress. He tried to force President Polk to admit that the "spot" where the shooting started was in Mexico. In Illinois the *State Register* called him "spotty Lincoln" and predicted his political death from "spotted fever."

THE SWEEP WESTWARD, THE LIFE HISTORY OF THE UNITED STATES

What causes a **mirage?**

The cause is simple: the bending and refracting of light waves by air layers of unequal density. The effect in a desert is not to be believed. A paved highway is coated with glistening "water," or a dry lake is filled to the brim, or lofty peaks turn into islands. Bushes and trees may be reflected in the surface of the conjured water, and the desert's heat shimmer may complete the illusion with convincing waves that lap at the shore.

THE DESERT, LIFE NATURE LIBRARY

Why will **missing-link** fossils never be found?

The bothersome misconception of a missing evolutionary link plagued anthropologists for decades. If men were men and apes were apes, it was argued, the connection could be proved by discovering a fossil that stood halfway between the two. Unfortunately for the early proponents of the theory of evolution, no missing-link fossils were found, nor would they ever be, for we know today that while both men and apes are descended from common ancestors, they bear the relationships of cousin to cousin and not grandparent to grandchild.

When did **modern man** emerge?

Although traces of modern man may go back as far as a couple of hundred thousand years, he cannot be said to have emerged in his present form until about 37,000 years ago. At this point people made their appearance who were virtually indistinguishable from those of today.

"Mohammed" or "Mehemet" or "Muhammad"?

The transliteration of Arabic words into English is a continuing problem for scholars. Not only does the pronunciation of Arabic vary throughout the Arab world, but several of the 28 letters of the Arabic alphabet represent sounds for which the English language has no exact equivalents.

Thus, so common an Arabic name as "Mohammed" has been variously spelled in English as "Muhammad," "Mohamed" and "Mehemet." None of these spellings give the exact equivalent of the Arab pronunciation.

THE ARAB WORLD, LIFE WORLD LIBRARY

What country has the most followers of **Mohammed?**

With some 85 million Moslems—about 90 per cent of the population—Indonesia is the largest Islamic land in the world. But the only mosque of any grandeur in all Southeast Asia looms with grotesque prominence in the tiny, oil-rich British protectorate of Brunei, on the northern coast of Borneo. Built a few years ago at a cost of $2.5 million by Sultan Sir Omar Ali Saifuddin Wasa'dul Khairi Waddin, Knight Commander of the Order of St. Michael and St. George—and named for himself—it has electric incense burners and an elevator to run the muezzin up the minaret from which he calls the faithful to prayer through a loudspeaker. SOUTHEAST ASIA, LIFE WORLD LIBRARY

Why is the **Monroe Doctrine** hated in Latin America?

President Theodore Roosevelt made the Doctrine anathema throughout Latin America in general—and Central America in particular—by promulgating what came to be known as the Theodore Roosevelt Corollary to the Doctrine. It had become customary for the Central American republics to borrow money from private bankers and then neglect to repay it. The U.S., argued Roosevelt, was morally obligated to collect such loans for European bankers since, under the Monroe Doctrine, Europeans were barred from using force to collect the money themselves. Under the Corollary, the U.S. on several occasions landed Marines in Honduras and Costa Rica. For years the Marines actually ruled Nicaragua.

CENTRAL AMERICA, LIFE WORLD LIBRARY

From the halls of **Montezuma**—or Moctezuma?

To Spaniards hearing the guttural Nahuatl language in the 16th Century, the name of the Aztec chief sounded like "Montezuma." This became common usage—and is so used in the hymn of the United States Marines. But experts today agree that "Moctezuma" is closer to the original Nahuatl. MEXICO, LIFE WORLD LIBRARY

*Why does the **moon** always keep the same face toward the earth?*

The modern explanation is, in part, that the moon is not a perfectly symmetrical spheroid. It has a massive bulge, which the earth's gravitation attracts like a plumb bob, thus keeping the same hemisphere pointing toward the earth.   PLANETS. LIFE SCIENCE LIBRARY

*How long did the **Moors** occupy Spain?*

For more than three centuries the greater part of Spain remained under Moslem rule. During all these years descendants of Visigoths and Hispano-Romans were united in the desire for reconquest—*Reconquista*. As early as 718 A.D. a Visigoth noble named Pelayo led the remnants of the Christian armies that had gathered in the mountains of Asturias into victorious battle against the Moslems. The *Reconquista* had begun. It did not end until Granada was conquered at the close of the Middle Ages, in 1492.   SPAIN. LIFE WORLD LIBRARY

Could *Moslem women* of the harem own property?

For 13 centuries Moslem women had one important advantage over their Western sisters: control over their own assets. Moslem women have always retained their property on getting married; this was their safeguard against divorce, which in Islam was very simple. A man had only to say three times the words, "I divorce you," and the marriage was at an end. But in such circumstances the woman retained the money and property she had brought with her, as well as the dowry that had been settled on her by her husband.   THE ARAB WORLD, LIFE WORLD LIBRARY

Why does a *moth* fly into a candle flame?

Moths are not "attracted" to light, as many people believe; their flight into the burning candle is simply their reaction to a stimulus. Long before man's artificial lights appeared on the planet, moths and other insects developed exceedingly involved mechanisms for navigation in relation to points of light—the sun and moon. The light rays from these distant sources are practically parallel when they reach the earth; the moth can navigate a straight line by always keeping the rays falling on its eyes at the same angle. However, if the source of light is nearby, as with a candle, the rays are not parallel, and the only way the moth can keep the angle roughly the same is by constantly changing its own direction toward the source of light. The result is a spiral path that eventually leads into the flame itself.   THE INSECTS, LIFE NATURE LIBRARY

Who was the first to climb a *mountain* for fun?

Among all the great events of the year 1492 there is one remembered chiefly by those for whom mountain climbing is a passion. In that historic year, Antoine de Ville, Chamberlain to King Charles VIII of France, obeyed His Majesty's royal command by leading a party of climbers to the top of Mont Aiguille. He even spent three days on its summit before coming down to write his "first, full, precise, and detailed account" of the first recorded attempt by man to climb a substantial mountain simply to get to the top. The first real outbreak of mountain climbing enthusiasm occurred before the middle of the 16th Century and included no less a personage than Leonardo da Vinci, who clambered up the southern slopes of the Pennines.   THE MOUNTAINS, LIFE NATURE LIBRARY

How dangerous is a *mountain lion?*

Known also as the cougar, panther, puma or catamount, this is the largest carnivore common to North America. Generations of American children have grown up in fear of this huge cat with its unearthly scream in the night. But the reputation it has as an attacker of man is greatly exaggerated. One did kill and eat a 13-year-old boy in Washington state in 1924, but that is the only such occurrence on record, and most naturalists are convinced that the few instances of cougars molesting people are the result of the cougars' suffering from rabies. THE MOUNTAINS, LIFE NATURE LIBRARY

Has *Mount Everest* been measured precisely?

Every recorded measurement of a large mountain may be from half a dozen to a few hundred feet in error. The point is emphasized by the way the first "official" height of Everest was arrived at in 1852. Measurements were made from six places. All were different, the lowest being 28,990 feet and the highest 29,026 feet. When all six were averaged, the figure came to exactly 29,000 feet. Unwilling to publish what they thought would seem like an estimate rather than an exact figure, the surveyors arbitrarily added two feet to make the official figure, 29,002 feet, sound better. It turned out to be 26 feet higher when measured by a party of Indians in 1954. Whatever its exact height, Everest is the world's highest mountain.

THE MOUNTAINS. LIFE NATURE LIBRARY

*Who was the first **movie star?***

Until 1910 performers were identified only as the "Biograph Girl" or the "Man with the Sad Eyes," etc. But when Carl Laemmle bought the contract of the "Biograph Girl," Florence Lawrence, he decided to advertise her by name and arranged for her to make a personal appearance in St. Louis. Adoring fans tore the buttons from her coat and box-office receipts soared; in short order nearly all producers copied Laemmle's example. Mary Pickford and Charlie Chaplin, the two most popular players, were able to demand and receive salaries of over $500,000 a year.

WAR, BOOM AND BUST. THE LIFE HISTORY OF THE UNITED STATES

*Where did the term **muckraker** come from?*

Journalism's most significant contribution to the progressive cause came through the exposé articles published by monthly magazines from 1902 on and circulated to a nationwide audience of the literate public. By 1906 President Theodore Roosevelt was able to speak of certain writers of political exposés who reminded him of Bunyan's Man with the Muck-rake, who, when offered a celestial crown, "would neither look up nor regard the crown he was offered, but continued to rake to himself the filth of the floor." T. R.'s label—muckraker—stuck. It was cherished, indeed, as a title of honor. THE PROGRESSIVE ERA. THE LIFE HISTORY OF THE UNITED STATES

How rapidly do single-celled creatures **multiply?**

The single-celled animal paramecium divides in two when it is about 22 hours old. In another 22 hours, each of these two animals will have grown to full size and is ready to divide again, and so on. If a solitary paramecium began to divide on January 1—and if all of its offspring survived—by March 7 its descendants would have a volume of a cubic mile. By April 12, their combined volume would be as large as the earth. Obviously no such population explosion could ever take place in nature—yet every species possesses a similar potential to grow and multiply fantastically. ECOLOGY. LIFE NATURE LIBRARY

What is the largest family of **musical instruments?**

The largest instrumental family is the percussion, a name derived from the Latin word meaning "to strike." Drums comprise the most important subdivision, but percussion instruments may include almost anything that makes a noise when hit. Serious composers have written parts for such "instruments" as typewriters and crashing chinaware, and one opera by Wagner calls for 18 anvils. SOUND AND HEARING. LIFE SCIENCE LIBRARY

N is for national anthem, nerve impulses and nirvana

Why do some men of Central America go by their "middle" names?

Proper names in Central America are composed of three elements: Christian name, father's family name and mother's family name. A man may use one or both family names. Carlos Castillo Armas, the late President of Guatemala, was usually called "Castillo Armas," seldom just "Castillo." But Anastasio Somoza Garcia, the late President of Nicaragua, was almost always called only "Somoza." A woman, when she marries, usually drops her mother's maiden name and adds her husband's family name, prefixed by "de," as in Lillian Somoza de Sevilla.

CENTRAL AMERICA, LIFE WORLD LIBRARY

What is the world's second largest nation?

Most strangers are unaware of Canada's sheer physical size. It is exceeded in area only by the Soviet Union. It has more lakes than the rest of the world combined. And while it contains one of the world's last great undeveloped areas, it is, paradoxically, the fifth largest trading nation on earth and has the third highest standard of living.

CANADA, LIFE WORLD LIBRARY

When did "The Star-Spangled Banner" become the **national anthem** of the United States?

It was not designated the national anthem until 1916 and was not confirmed by Congress until 1931. The words were inspired by U.S. valor under British bombardment (in the War of 1812), but the music, ironically, is from a British song, "To Anacreon in Heaven."

THE GROWING YEARS, THE LIFE HISTORY OF THE UNITED STATES

When did the first **Negro slaves** arrive in the U.S.?

"About the last of August came in a Dutch man of warre that sold us twenty negars." Thus concisely did John Rolfe, founder of commercial tobacco cultivation in Virginia, report the first importation in 1619 of Negroes from Africa.

THE NEW WORLD, THE LIFE HISTORY OF THE UNITED STATES

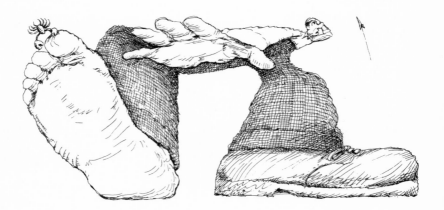

How fast do **nerve impulses** travel?

It was once thought that nerve impulses, the signals passed from one nerve cell to the next, were the swiftest phenomena in nature. Indeed, they may travel through nerve fibers at speeds as high as 200 miles an hour. But compared to modern technology, nerve cells are downright sluggish. If a crab nipped the toe of a 50-mile-high giant and a rocket were launched at the same instant, the pain would only be at his ankle when the rocket whooshed by his head.   THE CELL, LIFE SCIENCE LIBRARY

How much of the **Netherlands** is below sea level?

The Netherlands has been adding to its own land since the 13th Century by constructing an artificial coastland with dikes, then pumping out the impounded sea water with windmills and electric pumps. Today fully half of the Netherlands, including the two largest cities, lies below the level of the sea. An altimeter at the Amsterdam airport reads -13 feet; near Rotterdam it reads -30 feet.   WATER, LIFE SCIENCE LIBRARY

When is **Niagara Falls** likely to disappear?

The water dropping over Niagara digs great plunge pools at the base, undermining the shale cliff and causing the hard limestone cap to cave in. Niagara has eaten itself seven miles upstream since it was formed 10,000 years ago. At this rate, it will disappear into Lake Erie in 22,800 years.

WATER, LIFE SCIENCE LIBRARY

What is **nirvana?**

The Buddha believed that reincarnation could be avoided if a man followed a life of perfect justice and constant patience and kindness, renouncing all desire for worldly pleasures. He could then attain that release called nirvana. In the ancient Indian language of Sanskrit, nirvana means "final emancipation." In Buddhist thought, however, it does not signify an end of existence. Nirvana is, rather, an intangible, everlasting state of peace—"indescribable, inconceivable, ineffable." As the Buddha himself affirmed it, "Nirvana is bliss."   SOUTHEAST ASIA, LIFE WORLD LIBRARY

What was the first American **novel?**

In 1789 William Hill Brown, the son of a Boston clockmaker, wrote the first American novel, *The Power of Sympathy*. In subject matter, at least, the book seems closely akin to many of the modern novels now available at a corner drugstore, for it dealt with seduction, incest, abduction, rape and suicide.   NEW ENGLAND, TIME-LIFE LIBRARY OF AMERICA

O is for old wives' remedies, opera and outer space

What is the world's largest oasis?

It is the Nile valley, which runs 1,600 miles through an absolute desert and which drew to its fertile banks one of history's most impressive cultures, that of ancient Egypt. On the Sahara, that Texas of deserts where everything is bigger, there are a number of ribbon-like oases that stretch for 50 miles, and one, the "Street of Palms," that is 500 miles long. Other extensive oases are to be found on the banks of rivers like the Rio Grande, the Colorado, the Indus, the Tigris and the Euphrates.

THE DESERT, LIFE NATURE LIBRARY

Except for the tides, are ocean levels constant?

The ocean levels in the Northern Hemisphere drop eight inches every spring without any compensating rise south of the equator. No one knows where the water goes.

THE EARTH, LIFE NATURE LIBRARY

Where did the first **oil boom** begin?

Interest in oil's enormous commercial potential began only with a scientific paper in 1855 predicting that 90 per cent of crude oil could be distilled into salable products. With this impetus, the Seneca Oil Company was founded by a group of New York investors determined to look for oil by drilling, which had never been tried. Edwin L. Drake, a retired railroad conductor, was put in charge of operations. With an assistant he erected an enginehouse and derrick on a farm near Titusville, Pennsylvania, and on August 27, 1859, at a depth of 69.5 feet, oil began coming to the surface. Drake's well produced an unexpected nine gallons a day, which was hurriedly stored in tubs and whiskey barrels. Within 24 hours the boom was on. ENERGY, LIFE SCIENCE LIBRARY

What causes **old age**?

Old age results from a breakdown in the body's self-repair mechanisms. In nearly all organs, cells are constantly being used up and replaced; eventually, for reasons still unknown, the body becomes unable to replace the cells as fast as they die off. Muscles grow lean and stringy; heart, stomach and kidneys lose cells and perform less efficiently; brain cells vanish, taking memories with them. Drugs that could restore the body's capacity to repair itself would bring the human race close to immortality.

DRUGS, LIFE SCIENCE LIBRARY

How long did the **Old South** prosper?

The full, rich blooming of the Old South, the traditional South of the plantation, was a hothouse flowering that lasted a bare 20 years. Even for that brief period the Old South was less a fact than a dream, a Southern ideal based on the institution of slavery. The goal was to be a Southern version of the Greek city-state, with the equality of the master class guaranteed by the fact that even the lowest of them were superior to the most able slaves. THE GROWING YEARS, THE LIFE HISTORY OF THE UNITED STATES

Are "**old wives' remedies**" good for anything?

Folk medicine, despite its large humbug content, has proved so prolific a source of valuable drugs—quinine, opium, digitalis, reserpine—that mod-

99

ern scientists turn to it again and again for clues to the medications they seek. Though Ayurvedic physicians in India often recommend such exotic but useless remedies as diamond and ruby dust and rhinoceros horn, they were also among the first to use rauwolfia, from which came the first modern tranquilizers. DRUGS, LIFE SCIENCE LIBRARY

Was Olympia, site of the ancient games, dedicated to fair play?

Strangely enough, it was founded to commemorate a "fixed" race. Far from wishing to conceal the fact, the ancients celebrated it. Witness the huge and splendid pediment that still remains from the east gable of Olympia's Temple of Zeus. The hero of this sculpture, a prince named Pelops, was a schemer who secretly tampered with the wheel of his rival's chariot. At the first turn, off came the wheel; the chariot collapsed, the horses panicked and the driver was dragged to his death. Pelops, smiling, drove on to victory. Prospering mightily in the years that followed, he bequeathed his name to the whole region south of the Gulf of Corinth, the Peloponnesus. GREECE, LIFE WORLD LIBRARY

Who wrote the first opera?

The first opera, a tragedy called *Dafne* by Ottavio Rinuccini, which was set to music by Jacopo Peri, was performed in Florence about 1594. ITALY, LIFE WORLD LIBRARY

How large is an opossum at birth?

A baby possum is the size of a bee at birth and lives eight weeks inside its mother's marsupial pouch. THE FOREST, LIFE NATURE LIBRARY

Do opossums really "play possum"?

The classic example of the use of immobility as a survival technique is the death-feigning of the opossum. This animal, if attacked and frightened, sometimes falls down on its side in a position that most realistically resembles death. The withered-looking ears and bare tail are themselves suggestive of a corpse, and the opossum also draws back its lips to expose the teeth in a set grimace. The attacking animal, after a few sniffs at the prostrate body, will generally move away. THE MAMMALS, LIFE NATURE LIBRARY

*Why the name **Oriental Republic of Uruguay?***

This is the country's official name because it lies on the eastern, or "oriental," shore of the Uruguay River. *Orientales* is an old but still current term for the citizens of Uruguay. THE RIVER PLATE REPUBLICS. LIFE WORLD LIBRARY

*Where do **ostriches** roam?*

The ostrich, giant among living birds, lives the life of a grazing animal, roaming in little parties over the African veldt in the company of zebras, wildebeests and gazelles. Australia has its ratites, or ostrichlike birds—the emus and the cassowaries. But they are without the ostrich's plumage, and have even more rudimentary wings and a hairy, almost shaggy look.

THE BIRDS. LIFE NATURE LIBRARY

*Did the Turks of the **Ottoman Empire** persecute Christians and Jews?*

The Turks, contrary to the commonly held myth of the fanatical warriors of Islam, practiced a religious toleration remarkable for that or any age. Christians and Jews, in the eyes of the followers of the Koran, were like themselves "people of the book"; their option was to convert to Islam or not as they chose, as long as they paid a head tax incumbent on all nonbelievers.

THE BALKANS. LIFE WORLD LIBRARY

*How would we communicate with beings in **outer space?***

Some day, radio astronomers believe, one of their colleagues will experience the enormous excitement of receiving man's first message from intelligent beings on the planet of another star. Scientists have concluded that the one kind of message most likely to make sense to any intelligent form of life anywhere would be a mathematical one. An advanced extraterrestrial race might broadcast a simply coded bit of arithmetic. Once simple signals of this sort had been picked up and acknowledged, whole batches of mathematical facts and formulas could be exchanged to establish a basic vocabulary for further communications.

MATHEMATICS. LIFE SCIENCE LIBRARY

*How prevalent is **overweight** in the U.S.?*

The very abundance of foods that has solved the nutritional problems of the past has produced its own new set of problems. In the U.S., obesity is the most common nutritional disorder today. It has been estimated that one out of five American men, and one out of four women, are 10 per cent or more overweight.

HEALTH AND DISEASE. LIFE SCIENCE LIBRARY

*Do **owls** really see at night?*

Most owls, which hunt at night—because that is when the rodents they eat are abroad—have very large eyes packed with light-sensitive cells. This enables them to capture darting mice without hitting tree branches even in light no stronger than that produced by a candle burning 1,170 feet away.

THE FOREST. LIFE NATURE LIBRARY

P is for phrenology, Pony Express and pyrrhic victory

How large is the *Pampa*?

The Pampa, Argentina's heartland, spreads over an area of about 250,000 square miles, or 23 per cent of the nation. The Pampa was once the bed of an inland sea, and its deep alluvial soil is extremely fertile—perfect for wheat, corn and grazing grass. In the early 19th Century, enterprising Spanish, British, Italian and Irish immigrants carved out of the wilderness ranches, or *estancias,* so vast that the owners could gallop for days without coming to the end of their land. THE RIVER PLATE REPUBLICS, LIFE WORLD LIBRARY

Where do *Panama hats* come from?

For many years the fine hats woven by Ecuadorians from *toquilla* fiber had no easy access to the outside world. They were shipped to Panama for marketing and are consequently known around the world as Panama hats. THE ANDEAN REPUBLICS, LIFE WORLD LIBRARY

What *parliament* is the world's oldest?

It is the Althing of Iceland, originally established in the year 930. It shares power today with a popularly elected president.

SCANDINAVIA, LIFE WORLD LIBRARY

Do all *penguins* live near the South Pole?

Most of these natty birds do live in the cold wastes of the Antarctic ice, but a maverick colony of about 250 individuals lives in the Galápagos Islands, astride the equator.

THE BIRDS, LIFE NATURE LIBRARY

What is a Caribbean *pepper pot?*

This delightful culinary artifact was developed in the days before refrigeration to preserve meat and poultry more easily than could be done through smoking or salting; it survives its obsolescence because it tastes so good. The food is put into a big kettle with hot peppers and the juice of cassava root and set on the back of the stove to simmer. New ingredients are added as they come to hand, and the contents are eaten in small quantities, so that the pot never becomes empty. The simmering of years adds to the richness and savor. A good pepper pot is so highly valued that it may be willed from generation to generation.

THE WEST INDIES, LIFE WORLD LIBRARY

What was *phrenology?*

In the almost total absence of experimental brain research, speculation developed in the late 18th Century in the elaborate nonsense known as phrenology. It began with a Viennese physiologist, Franz Joseph Gall, who assumed that the bumps on a man's skull represented various areas of his brain that had been particularly well developed. His assumption was completely unfounded, for there is no relation between the brain's bumps and those of the skull. Nevertheless, Gall believed that a man's personality could be deduced by a "reading" of his skull bumps. He divided the brain into 37 areas, identifying each area with such traits as "moral taste," "self-esteem" and "duty." His ideas achieved enormous popularity. Europeans flocked to have their skulls read, and phrenological societies flourished in the wake of Gall's lecture tours. THE MIND, LIFE SCIENCE LIBRARY

What is **Picasso's** full name?

He was baptized Pablo Diego José Francisco de Paula Juan Nepomuceno María de los Remedios Cipriano de la Santísima Trinidad—a roster of names that honored various godparents, relatives and saints. At the end of this long string came two more names, Ruiz and Picasso—the first for his father and the second for his mother, as is Spanish custom. Picasso signed himself P. Ruiz or P. Ruiz Picasso until about 1902, when he settled on Picasso alone—partly because it was less common than Ruiz, partly out of fondness for his mother.   THE WORLD OF PICASSO. TIME-LIFE LIBRARY OF ART

Is **planned obsolescence** a modern concept?

The idea existed long before the phrase was coined. Alexis de Tocqueville, the uncannily perceptive Frenchman who wrote *Democracy in America* (1835), was told by an American sailor that ships in the United States were built to last only a few years: their design would be out-of-date by the time they were worn out.   THE UNITED STATES. LIFE WORLD LIBRARY

Why does a house **plant** turn toward the light?

The plant does not seek out the light. What happens is that the light re-
duces the concentration of a growth hormone, auxin, on the bright side
of the stem. As a result, the dark side grows more rapidly, bending the
stem toward the light. Similarly, a gnarled old oak, though it may bear
700,000 leaves, manages to keep them all out of each other's way so
that there is a minimum of shading of one leaf by another.

THE FOREST, LIFE NATURE LIBRARY

Do **plants** breathe?

The energy-trapping process of photosynthesis occurs only in plants.
The energy-*releasing* process of respiration, however, occurs in both
plants and animals. During the day, when plenty of light is available,
plants carry on photosynthesis and respiration at the same time. But
they do considerably more photosynthesizing than they do respirating.
That is why plants can produce food for themselves and still provide
enough for the whole animal kingdom as well. It is also why plants can

use oxygen for their own respiration and still have enough left over to distribute into the air for animals to breathe.   THE CELL, LIFE SCIENCE LIBRARY

How old are *plastics?*

The first modern plastic was celluloid, an inflammable amalgam of cellulose, nitric acid and camphor invented in 1868 by John Wesley Hyatt. By the end of the century it was being molded into dice, dominoes, "rubber" stamps and even medals for Coxey's Army. But consumers were sometimes seared by blazing celluloid collars and eyeglass frames, and by the 1950s it had been largely displaced by cheaper, safer petroleum-based plastics.   GIANT MOLECULES, LIFE SCIENCE LIBRARY

How successful was the *Pony Express?*

The Pony Express, established in 1860 by the great freighting company of Russell, Majors and Waddell, carried only mail. Whereas a stagecoach could average 100 to 125 miles every 24 hours, the pony rider covered 250 miles. Relays of riders flew all the way from St. Joseph, Missouri, to

Sacramento in 10 days. But the Pony Express never turned a profit; the experiment lasted only 18 months. THE UNION SUNDERED, THE LIFE HISTORY OF THE UNITED STATES

What country has the world's densest *population?*

Holland is the most densely populated nation, with nearly 12 million people—896 per square mile. The population has more than doubled so far in the 20th Century, and if the rate of growth remains the same, as seems likely, the present 12 million will become 18 to 20 million before the beginning of the 21st Century. THE LOW COUNTRIES, LIFE WORLD LIBRARY

How extensive is the *population explosion* in Southeast Asia?

Europe's large-scale colonial exploitation of the area introduced public health measures that in time resulted in a single startling statistic: Southeast Asia's population has increased twentyfold in the past 150 years.

SOUTHEAST ASIA, LIFE WORLD LIBRARY

What is the world's busiest port?

New York, long the biggest port in the world, fell to second place in 1962 when it handled 93 million tons of cargo to Rotterdam's 96 million. Some 25,000 seagoing vessels and 250,000 barges and other small craft enter and leave Rotterdam each year. Second to Rotterdam in Europe is London. THE LOW COUNTRIES, LIFE WORLD LIBRARY

What is a "preacher bird"?

The red-eyed vireo won that nickname with the monotonous repetition of its song. One male is reported to have repeated its refrain 22,197 times between dawn and dark, a record not likely to be challenged except by another red-eyed vireo. THE BIRDS, LIFE NATURE LIBRARY

What are the best clues to prehistoric man?

For almost two million years, man's ability to make stone tools enabled him to exploit and finally dominate his environment. With tools he fought enemies, hunted food, made clothing, built shelters and fashioned art. Because stone implements are so durable, they are often the evidence most found by paleoanthropologists and are essential in the recreation of the activities of prehistoric peoples. EARLY MAN, LIFE NATURE LIBRARY

Why does Australia retain more primitive animals than any other continent?

Australia in geologic terms is an ancient land, perhaps one of the most ancient. It was isolated from other continents in prehistoric eras; the "alpine storms" that threw up the mighty mountain ranges of all the other continents passed Australia by. Hence Australia has a near-monopoly of primitive marsupials, animals that carry their young in a pouch. Largest marsupial is the kangaroo, which, with the ostrichlike emu, forms Australia's coat of arms. Most bizarre of all Australia's creatures is the duck-billed platypus, which stands between the modern mammal and the creatures of prehistory. It has a ducklike bill, webbed feet and a fur coat, and is amphibious. It hatches its young from eggs, then suckles them. Among a profusion of reptiles, there is the goanna, a six-foot-long "dragon" of repellent aspect, which, if it suddenly meets a horse—or a human being—is likely to mistake it for a tree and try to claw its way up for safety, with embarrassing results. AUSTRALIA AND NEW ZEALAND. LIFE WORLD LIBRARY

Why are Britain's **private schools** called "public"?

Now almost wholly private in every sense of the word, Britain's public schools are so named because originally they were just that—schools for the ordinary and often underprivileged public of the towns where they were founded. Winchester, founded in 1382 as "Seint Marie College at Wynchester," and Eton, established in 1440 by King Henry VI as "the King's College of Our Lady of Eton Beside Windsor," long had more poor students on scholarships than sons of rich aristocrats and landed gentlemen. BRITAIN. LIFE WORLD LIBRARY

Why are plants a poor source of **protein?**

At some point in its life a newly divided plant cell stops dividing and starts to blow up like a balloon. This enlargement accounts for more than 90 per cent of the growth we observe. The protoplasm, whose volume usually remains unchanged during this inflation, is spread out more and more thinly against the plant walls. In this type of growth by enlargement, plant cells are very different from animal cells, which grow exclusively by division and remain always filled with protoplasm. This is why animal cells—i.e., meat—are always high in protein. In plants, by contrast, only the young cells, such as wheat germ and nuts or growing shoots of bamboo and palm heart, are high in protein.

THE PLANTS. LIFE NATURE LIBRARY

How did the term "pyrrhic victory" originate?

After the early death of Alexander the Great, his empire fell apart, dividing roughly along continental lines. Greece fell to a succession of native warlords. The most ambitious of these was Pyrrhus, the King of Epirus, who undertook to contest Europe's future with Rome. In 279 B.C. Pyrrhus won a bloody battle on Italian soil. Viewing the carnage, he remarked to his officers, "Another victory like this and I am lost!"

GREECE. LIFE WORLD LIBRARY

110

R is for rain, Renaissance and Babe Ruth

Who discovered *radioactivity?*

In 1896 in Paris, Henri Becquerel noticed that uranium, with no external stimulation, emitted radiation that would fog a film just as X-rays did. Thus was radioactivity discovered, and it launched the extraordinary careers of Pierre and Marie Curie, who shared with Becquerel a Nobel Prize for the discovery. The Curies went on with more intensive research and in 1898 discovered radium and polonium, by far the most radioactive elements then known. For this Marie won another Nobel Prize and became the only person ever to be so honored twice.

MATTER, LIFE SCIENCE LIBRARY

What do *radio astronomers* hear?

For the fun of it, radio astronomers occasionally connect their antennae and amplifiers to loudspeakers so they can hear the cosmic broadcasts as audible sound waves. They say that when they do, the Milky Way hisses incessantly, the sun sighs intermittently and the planet Jupiter comes through with a deep, lugubrious grumble that sounds like the ancient Roman god of thunder himself. Actually, radio astronomers "listen" to the universe only through the graphs of signal intensity traced by their monitoring instruments as their antennae sweep the sky. By marking the strength and direction of radio hot spots, they have accumulated a picture of the radio heavens altogether different from the picture of the optical heavens seen by ordinary astronomers. THE UNIVERSE, LIFE NATURE LIBRARY

Where was the first transcontinental *railroad* completed?

On May 10, 1869, a hitherto obscure spot in the Utah wilderness—Promontory, 53 miles northwest of Ogden—attained a unique place in American history. There two railroad engines, the Central Pacific's *Jupiter* out of Sacramento and the Union Pacific's *No. 119* from Omaha, touched cowcatchers. This odd confrontation marked the completion of the first transcontinental railroad, and the event was celebrated with appropriate symbolism. The final tie was of polished laurel wood, and a final spike of gold was driven into place by a silver-plated hammer. Promontory was bypassed by a new line in 1904.

THE UNION RESTORED, THE LIFE HISTORY OF THE UNITED STATES

Does cloud-seeding make *rain*?

Meteorologists are now persuaded that almost all precipitation except tropical rain begins as rapidly fattening ice crystals. The ice-crystal theory of rain led to man's most hopeful attempts to influence the behavior of clouds since primitive man danced his first rain dance. The artificial seeding of rain clouds was developed in 1946 by General Electric's Vincent J. Schaefer and Irving Langmuir. The principle behind it seems a model of logic and simplicity: to introduce into a cloud of supercooled droplets an agent that promotes the formation of ice crystals. Artificial seeding was launched in a wave of optimism. By now, however, years of experience have led to a more hardheaded evaluation of rainmaking's effectiveness. The truth is that when rainfall in seeded areas is carefully compared with rainfall in "control" areas, it is almost impossible to tell whether the cloud produced rain because it was seeded or because it was about to rain anyway. WEATHER, LIFE SCIENCE LIBRARY

How dense is a tropical **rain forest**?

The "jungle" of storybooks is found only in a rain forest that has been disturbed by man or that borders stream courses and forest margins where sunlight produces rank growth. In undisturbed rain forests, the canopy of leaves is so thick that even in the middle of the day the light is reminiscent of Temperate Zone twilight. This scarcity of light suppresses most of the undergrowth. As a result, between the colonnades of the trunks the forest aisles are comparatively open. THE FOREST, LIFE NATURE LIBRARY

What is the **rainiest spot** on earth?

The amount of rainfall varies from less than an inch a year in some desert areas to the torrential 470 inches that pour down each year, on the average, on Mount Waialeale in Hawaii. In the U.S., the spread ranges from a meager 1.7 inches in California's Death Valley to a copious 140 to 150 inches in coastal areas of the Pacific Northwest, only 800 miles away. WEATHER, LIFE SCIENCE LIBRARY

How near are the **redwood forests** to depletion?

At the time Columbus found America, redwoods, which grow 300 feet tall and can live 2,000 years, covered some 1.5 million acres of what was to become California. Most have since been felled; little more than 100,-000 acres of them are now protected in parks.

THE PACIFIC STATES, TIME-LIFE LIBRARY OF AMERICA

How did the **Renaissance** end?

In 1519 the remarkable Charles V of Spain became Holy Roman Emperor. Charles was a religious zealot who was determined to stamp out Martin Luther's heresy. He was equally determined to extend the power of Hapsburg Spain. At first, he received political support from the Medici Pope Clement VII, but when Clement intrigued against him, Charles sent his forces into Italy. In 1527 Rome was sacked, and the heavy hand of Spain and the Inquisition closed over Italy. The freedom of thought that had been the mental base of the Renaissance was toppled; almost simultaneously the commerce of Italy, which had supplied men with the leisure and the wealth to support the arts, dwindled as trade routes shifted to the Atlantic and the New World. The Renaissance was over.

ITALY. LIFE WORLD LIBRARY

Did a majority of the American colonists back the **Revolution?**

John Adams put the Tories (also called the Loyalists) at one third of the population; he gave another third to the fence-sitters. While contemporaries and later historians have argued about which side had the numerical preponderance—and the argument still goes on—one fact is clear: a substantial portion of the American people opposed the war and its objectives, and another large, if fluctuating, number switched from one side to the other as the fortunes of war changed.

THE MAKING OF A NATION. THE LIFE HISTORY OF THE UNITED STATES

What kind of horns do **rhinoceroses** grow?

There are two forms of rhinoceroses in Africa and three in Asia, all characterized by exceptionally thick skins and the presence of a varying number of "horns" on their snouts. These horns are of a very special type, consisting of a rigid pyramid of closely impacted hair.

THE MAMMALS. LIFE NATURE LIBRARY

How long is South America's **River Plate?**

The River Plate, which the Spanish-speaking people call the Río de la Plata, is one of the great waterways of the world and, like the Danube and the Mississippi, has had a profound effect on the vast area that forms its basin. Yet, strictly speaking, it is not a river at all but a wide estuary fed by the Uruguay and Paraná Rivers and their tributaries. The River Plate itself stretches only a little more than 150 miles between the confluence of its parent streams and the South Atlantic.

THE RIVER PLATE REPUBLICS, LIFE WORLD LIBRARY

*How did the word "**robot**" enter the language?*

Rossum's Universal Robots (R.U.R.), a play by Czechoslovakia's Karel Capek, was a New York stage success in 1922. In it the near-human robots revolt against man's domination and take over the world. The new word (from the Czech word *robata*, or "forced labor") was introduced into the English language and spawned a new idea: that man might eventually be destroyed by forcing other beings to do his tasks.

EASTERN EUROPE, LIFE WORLD LIBRARY

*Is the name of the country more properly **Romania** or **Rumania**?*

There is considerable disagreement over the spelling of "Romania." "Roumania," which is sometimes seen in English, is the French spelling.

"Rumania" is generally used elsewhere in Europe. The Romanians themselves, however, favor the "o" spelling to point out that they are not
Slavs, like their neighbors, and to imply that they are descendants of the
Roman conquerors of Transylvania and the Dacians, the original inhab-
itants of the area. Hungarians, who long quarreled with Romania over
Transylvania, maintain that the Dacians were killed by the Romans and
that any possible survivors withdrew with the Romans in the Third Century before barbarian onslaughts. THE BALKANS. LIFE WORLD LIBRARY

What was the major cause of the fall of **Rome**?

Edward Gibbon, the masterful British scholar who spent a lifetime
producing *The Decline and Fall of the Roman Empire,* thought the
most important factor was the rise of Christianity. Summarizing Gibbon's point of view, the popular American historian Will Durant
wrote in *Caesar and Christ:* "[Christianity] had declared war upon the
classic culture. . . . It turned men's thoughts from . . . this world
. . . and had lured them into seeking individual salvation through as-
ceticism and prayer, rather than collective salvation through devotion
to the state. . . . It had preached an ethic of nonresistance and peace
when the survival of the Empire had demanded a will to war. Christ's victory had been Rome's death." ITALY. LIFE WORLD LIBRARY

How widespread is the production of **Roquefort cheese**?

By French law only the cheese actually produced within the town of
Roquefort itself can be sold under that designation. FRANCE. LIFE WORLD LIBRARY

How did **rubber** get its name?

The first pieces of rubber ever seen in Europe were probably some oddly
bouncing balls brought from Haiti by Christopher Columbus in 1496.
In the Amazon Valley, however, the people used caoutchouc, as they
called the substance, for a good deal more than amusement. By spread-
ing a thin film of the sap of the hovea tree on cloth and then hardening it
by exposure to sunlight or smoke, they fabricated crude waterproof gar-
ments. They also made bottles from the sap (now called latex), and even
anticipated present-day expensive "molded" shoes by pouring the latex
on their feet and legs and letting it dry into waterproof boots. However,

Joseph Priestley, the great 18th Century English chemist, apparently ignored these significant qualities of the material—its elasticity, flexibility and impermeability—when he gave it its English name. It was "excellently adapted," he noted, "to the purpose of wiping from paper the marks of a black lead pencil," i.e., by rubbing. And because it came from the West Indies, it received the name "India rubber."

GIANT MOLECULES, LIFE SCIENCE LIBRARY

Which is the oldest city in Russia?

That honor belongs to Kiev, now the provincial capital of the Ukraine but once the center of a vast realm that reached as far as the Volga River in the northeast. It was in Kiev that Russia's last pagan ruler, Vladimir I, was baptized in the 10th Century and from which he requested the Patriarch of Constantinople to send out missionaries to Christianize his subjects. The rulers of Kiev dominated Russia for almost 300 years, but at the end of the 12th Century their leadership passed to princes of the north and eventually to the Muscovites.

RUSSIA, LIFE WORLD LIBRARY

Do any Russians own their land?

The last remnants of private property, the plots allotted to peasants, now constitute slightly more than 3 per cent of the total agricultural land. But they produce about half of the gross agricultural output, including almost half of the livestock products.

RUSSIA, LIFE WORLD LIBRARY

What did Babe Ruth think of his record-breaking salary?

When Ruth was chided about the fact that his $80,000 salary was higher than President Herbert Hoover's, he is supposed to have observed, after a moment's meditation, "Well, I had a better year."

WAR, BOOM AND BUST, THE LIFE HISTORY OF THE UNITED STATES

S is for Santa Claus, sex and Sitting Bull

*How does a **salmon** find its way home to spawn?*

The research literature of fisheries is replete with observations and speculation about the manner in which salmon come home to their rivers from the high seas. It has been variously suggested that they follow currents, guide themselves by the sun using polarized light like bees, even use sights on the stars, or perhaps have a directional memory. None of these suggestions is necessarily foolish. But a University of Rhode Island scientist has developed a provocative new theory, using an electronic computer to perform the tedious calculations required. His findings strongly suggest that salmon may actually have only a minimum of the directional, or navigational, sense they have always been credited with. Actually, according to this theory, they may swim quite randomly on their return—but such are their numbers that enough of them always hit the general vicinity of their parent river to complete the spawning run. Once in coastal waters, the salmon can accomplish the rest of the trip quite easily. All rivers, and even their tributary streams, are believed to have a characteristic odor that the fish can recognize, even though it may be very weak. THE FISHES. LIFE NATURE LIBRARY

*Where does all the **salt** in the sea come from?*

Part of it has come from the breaking up of rocks by frost and erosion, the gradual wearing away of mountains, which releases locked-in chemicals and permits them to be carried down to the ocean in solution by rain water. The rest has come from rocks beneath the ocean bed. There has been a constant slow addition to the sea's salinity over hundreds of millions of years. There is a curious way of deducing this: the body cells of animals (including fish) have a lower salt content than sea water has. From this it is possible to conclude that sea water, at the time life first took shape, was less salty than it is now. THE SEA. LIFE NATURE LIBRARY

*Are **sandstorms** and duststorms similar?*

Both are whipped up by robust winds. But dust particles, forming clouds so thick they blot out the sun, can be lifted thousands of feet into the air by a good blow, while sand, being heavier and coarser, rarely gets more than a few feet off the ground. A sandstorm often starts with a mist of suspended dust and sand. When the mist clears, the heavier particles remain as a low, thick cloud, gliding over the desert like a great moving carpet. The air above is clear, and the heads of people (and of ostriches, which are ideally constructed to survive sandstorms) project out of the cloud as if they were walking chin-deep in water. The abrasive, sandblast effect of the blown sand is greatest at ground level and insignificant above a height of 18 inches. THE DESERT. LIFE NATURE LIBRARY

*How did **Santa Claus** originate?*

Nicholas, a Near Eastern saint, became the guardian of sailors in the 11th Century. By the 13th Century, seagoing Dutchmen had built 23 churches in his honor. It was in the 14th Century that the saint became associated with children and gift-giving when the choir boys of Holland's many Saint Nicholas churches began parading through the streets begging for "bishop money" on December 6, the supposed birthday of the saint. The Dutch settlers brought their Saint Nicholas (nicknamed

Sinterklaas) to America. Later he merged with the merry, Falstaffian Father Christmas brought over by English settlers, and his name became Santa Claus, an Anglicized version of his Dutch nickname.

THE LOW COUNTRIES, LIFE WORLD LIBRARY

How high must a *satellite* fly to stay in orbit?

The lifetime of a satellite is determined by its closest approach to earth (its perigee height). If it comes within 80 to 100 miles, air drag will bring it down in a few days, and final disintegration will occur at an altitude of about 50 miles.

MAN AND SPACE, LIFE SCIENCE LIBRARY

How many branches of *science* exist?

At last count, the number of branches of science listed by the National Science Foundation had reached 620. But most of the "ologies" of today are merely new subdivisions in the four main provinces of thought that were in evidence as long ago as the Stone Age: mathematics, which has to do with the relationships between numbers, shapes and other logical symbols; the physical sciences, which deal with the inanimate constituents of the universe; the life, or biological, sciences, which deal with living matter; and the social sciences, which are concerned with human conduct, collective as well as individual.

THE SCIENTIST, LIFE SCIENCE LIBRARY

How does the number of *scientists* at work today compare with the number of scientists in earlier centuries?

Since the Renaissance, the world's population has doubled and redoubled. Over approximately the same period, the scientific community has multiplied a hundredfold in each century: from a platoon counted in individuals in 1670, to a regiment counted in hundreds in 1770, to a division counted in ten thousands in 1870, to an army estimated at six million today. This phenomenal rate of proliferation has meant that the number of scientists living at any one time has constituted 90 per cent of the total number of scientists who ever lived up to that time. As a corollary, it can be reasonably estimated that nine tenths of current scientific knowledge was yet to be created when our present elder statesmen of the scientific community were graduated from college in the 1920s.

THE SCIENTIST, LIFE SCIENCE LIBRARY

How large is the sea?

There is enough water in the sea to fill a standpipe 75 miles in diameter and 70,000 miles high—which is approximately one third the distance to the moon. The sea contains 330 million cubic miles of water; the volume of all land above sea level is only one eighteenth as great. If all the irregularities on the earth's surface were to be smoothed out, both above and below the water, no land would show at all. The ocean would cover the globe to a depth of 12,000 feet. THE SEA, LIFE NATURE LIBRARY

Do baby sea lions swim instinctively?

Sea-lion pups are born early in the summer, one to a cow, after a 12-month gestation period. Like all mammals, they must be suckled by their mothers and taught to fend for themselves. They do not know how to swim when they are born and probably learn by following their mothers through the surf into the sea. ECOLOGY, LIFE NATURE LIBRARY

What great contribution to mankind was made by **Ignaz Semmelweis**?

A Hungarian-born obstetrician, Semmelweis took a post at a Vienna hospital in 1846. He noted that in one ward, tended by students fresh from dissecting cadavers, one patient in eight died of puerperal fever. In another, ministered by midwives who were not thus contaminated, the death rate was much lower. Semmelweis ordered all attendants to wash their hands in chlorinated water. A year later the death rate in his ward had dropped almost to zero. Though scoffed and ignored at the time, he was among the first to detect a correlation between filth and disease.

HEALTH AND DISEASE, LIFE SCIENCE LIBRARY

How much can the *senses* be sharpened?

Some of the world's more specialized vocations indicate that man can develop his senses into a phenomenal means for measuring nuances. A vintner can taste the amounts of alcohol or acidity in a wine to within 1 per cent. Color technicians can see a difference between shades of red indistinguishable to the layman. A baker kneading dough can feel its moisture content within 2 per cent.

THE BODY, LIFE SCIENCE LIBRARY

Why do *sequoia trees* live so long?

Sequoias live upward of 3,000 years and are among the oldest of living things. Their longevity is largely due to the extraordinary qualities of sequoia bark. It is too thick (sometimes up to two feet) and too highly flavored with tannin to be vulnerable to attack by any known species of insect. Spongy and fibrous, it is nearly as fireproof as asbestos. About the only things that can threaten a mature sequoia are a change of climate, earthquakes and erosion. A giant sequoia may begin to bear seeds when it is 70 years of age, but it is not usually mature until it is 300 or more years old. THE FOREST, LIFE NATURE LIBRARY

*What was the **Seraglio** in the Ottoman Empire?*

A term applied by Turks to the Sultan's entire household, court and palace, the word was used by Europeans to refer specifically to the elaborately organized women's quarters within the palace. The Seraglio was ruled by the Sultan's mother, who supervised a vast array of disciplinary and administrative officers, as well as eunuchs who were held responsible for se-

123

curity. The women who lived in the imperial harem—sometimes num-
bering as many as 1,200—were mostly slaves and were rarely bound to
the Sultan in legal marriage. TURKEY, LIFE WORLD LIBRARY

Is a father or mother responsible for a child's **sex**?

When sperm and egg fuse, the father's contribution to his offspring is primarily in the genetic material contained in the head of the sperm. It is
this contribution that determines the infant's sex. GROWTH, LIFE SCIENCE LIBRARY

Can an infant's **sex** be predicted before birth?

The answer to the question "Will the baby be a boy or a girl?" will probably remain concealed until the moment of birth. If the physician suspects
a congenital malformation in the baby, he may test his suspicion by taking a sample of the amniotic fluid. Because this fluid contains a few of
the baby's cells, he may then be able to determine the infant's sex. But
the amniotic fluid is rarely sampled, so conjecture is all that is left.

GROWTH, LIFE SCIENCE LIBRARY

How did the **Shakers** get their name?

The Shakers danced their religious services. They formed two lines, fore-
arms out and hands hanging, then they moved in rhythm toward and
away from one another. As they danced they sang religious songs. One
was a hymn that went: "With ev'ry gift I will unite, And join in sweet devotion, To worship God is my delight, With hands and feet in motion."

THE SWEEP WESTWARD, THE LIFE HISTORY OF THE UNITED STATES

Where does a **shark** have teeth in addition to its mouth?

Inside a shark's mouth are row upon row of teeth for seizing, shearing,
piercing or crunching—teeth that renew themselves like dragon seed,
moving forward to replace those that are worn out, get torn out or fall
out with age. These teeth are actually specialized versions of the thousands of "teeth" with which the shark's entire skin is covered—tiny, razor-
sharp, close-set denticles that can flay a swimmer with a single sideways
swipe. Coated with hard dentine, these rasplike scales once made a fine
abrasive for cabinetmakers. THE FISHES, LIFE NATURE LIBRARY

Are sharks really dangerous?

Sharks are just about the only creatures left in nature that will attack men without provocation. In World War II a training manual that the U.S. Navy issued to men serving in shark-infested areas played down the menace of the shark. An article in a national magazine debunked the shark and portrayed it as cowardly—easy to scare off with a shout or a swat on the snout. This notion is false. Sharks each year make at least several dozen proved attacks on human beings that end in death or maiming. In one place alone—the waters along Australia's east coast—more than 200 authenticated shark attacks on human beings have been recorded in 150 years.   THE SEA, LIFE NATURE LIBRARY

Do shock treatments cure mental illness?

Shock does not cure a patient. It simply relieves his symptoms temporarily, bringing him back to reality so that he can be receptive to various forms of psychotherapy. In recent years shock therapy has been almost entirely replaced by the use of the new tranquilizers and antidepressant drugs.   THE MIND, LIFE SCIENCE LIBRARY

How did the **shoeshine** start?

A high polish on shoes is a tradition passed down from the Spanish *caballero* (gentleman on horseback), whose shiny boots served notice that he rode his own horse and did not walk along dusty roads with lesser men. SPAIN, LIFE WORLD LIBRARY

When was the first **shopping center** built?

In 1928 a group of businessmen in Ardmore, Pennsylvania, bought up a 20-acre estate on which they built the first complete shopping complex outside a major city. They called it Suburban Square, and it contained two major department stores, an embryo supermarket, doctors' offices, a movie theater, three clothing stores, a bookshop, a record shop and a dozen other stores. Since then the suburban shopping center has become a national institution. WHEELS, LIFE SCIENCE LIBRARY

*Which eats more, a **shrew** or a **python**?*

Mammals, with fur and a layer of subcutaneous fat to help retain body heat, plus a high rate of metabolism for the continued production of heat, can stand extremes of cold almost indefinitely, but they give up a certain elasticity in the process. They require a steady supply of food to keep their internal fires stoked. An extreme example is the shrew, which must eat heartily every hour or two, or it will starve to death. By contrast, a python needs a good meal only about once a year.

THE EARTH, LIFE NATURE LIBRARY

*Did **Sitting Bull** win the battle of Little Bighorn?*

Even though legend places Sitting Bull at the head of the Sioux who wiped out Lieutenant Colonel George Custer and his men, he was actually a medicine man who stayed behind the lines during the melee; two other war chiefs, Crazy Horse and Gall, won the battle.

THE AGE OF STEEL AND STEAM, THE LIFE HISTORY OF THE UNITED STATES

*Does a fish have a **sixth sense**?*

Any home fish tank or big-city aquarium offers practical and striking proof of the unique sixth sense possessed by fishes: the lateral line sensory system that steers them unerringly away from the invisible glass walls. Outwardly visible to a greater or lesser degree in all fishes as a line extending along each side of the body to the tail, these sensory organs function in an intermediate area between hearing and touch. After long scientific debate, it is now established that they are sensitive to low-frequency vibrations and pressure waves built up as the fish passes rocks and other barriers, or sent out by waves and currents or by movements of solid objects under water.

THE FISHES, LIFE NATURE LIBRARY

*Who introduced **skiing** to Switzerland?*

Skis were long used in Scandinavia. A Norwegian demonstrated the use of skis in Winterthur, Switzerland, in 1889, but it remained for the British to popularize the sport. In 1894 Sir Arthur Conan Doyle, creator of Sherlock Holmes, published his account of a Swiss ski journey, and after that, Englishmen introduced skiing at Grindelwald in the canton of Bern

and at Davos and St. Moritz in the Grisons. Today, it is estimated, half
the adults in Switzerland are skiers.   SWITZERLAND. LIFE WORLD LIBRARY

Where was the first skyscraper built?

In 1885, Chicago completed a building rising a full 10 stories above
street level. This elevation, breathtaking for its time, was made possible
by a new technique adopted by the architect William Jenney in which a
metal framework supported floors and masonry walls. Since the masonry
bore no weight, it could be built upward to almost any height. Within a
few years such architects as Daniel Burnham, John Root and Louis Sul-
livan had made Chicago the birthplace of the skyscraper.

REACHING FOR EMPIRE, THE LIFE HISTORY OF THE UNITED STATES

How many primary smells exist?

The chemistry and physics of smell are not well defined, but one recent
classification considers every odor a blend of four primary smells—fra-
grant, acid, rancid and burnt. If these primary smells could be measured
on an arbitrary scale, every odor on earth could be given a distinctive number based on the strength of its four constituents.   THE BODY, LIFE SCIENCE LIBRARY

Why does a snake have a forked tongue?

The tines of a snake's tongue send samples of air to a pair of spherical
chambers in the mouth called Jacobsen's organs. The chambers are lined
with sensory cells that have nervous connections with the olfactory lobes
of the brain. When a snake flicks its forked tongue, it is testing for
odors; the nostrils are not believed to contribute much to the sense of
smell. Snake behavior largely consists of automatic reactions to odors.

THE DESERT, LIFE NATURE LIBRARY

Which snakes are the most poisonous, cobras or rattlesnakes?

The prize has usually gone to cobras, because when white rats are in-
jected with equal amounts of cobra and rattler venom, the cobra-injected
animal dies first. The true answer, however, is that both are deadly; it all
depends on whether one prefers to die by paralysis (cobras) or by having
one's tissues destroyed (rattlers).   THE REPTILES, LIFE NATURE LIBRARY

*How might **Sodom and Gomorrah** have been destroyed?*

Modern Sodom is today the lowest peopled place on earth, 1,286 feet below sea level. Extensive natural gas reserves were discovered in its vicinity in 1957 and are now being exploited. The discovery of these reserves gave rise to the theory that the mysterious destruction of Sodom and its twin city, Gomorrah, in the Bible might actually have been brought about by explosions of just such gas as is being exploited today.

ISRAEL, LIFE WORLD LIBRARY

*What portion of the population of **South Africa** is nonwhite?*

More than 80 per cent, including Africans (68.2 per cent), Coloreds (9.77 per cent) and Asians (3 per cent). The Coloreds are people of mixed ancestry.

SOUTH AFRICA, LIFE WORLD LIBRARY

Are the whites of **South Africa** *socially and politically united?*

Though they work together in business or farming and cooperate in some aspects of public work, the two groups—Afrikaans-speaking and English-speaking—have not really merged. Differences of language, religion and culture have remained almost as sharp as they were at the passing in 1909 of the Act of Union, which, it was hoped, would lead to a steady coalescing of the two peoples. Even of social contact there is astonishingly little, and in recent years the Nationalist Government has deliberately put a stop—in the interest of keeping the Dutch-descended ruling group uncontaminated—to all attempts to bring the two peoples together through common schooling.   SOUTH AFRICA, LIFE WORLD LIBRARY

What is the largest city in **South America?**

It is São Paulo, Brazil, a burgeoning center of commerce and industry southwest of Rio de Janeiro. It was a quiet town of 25,000 people only 80 years ago. Today it covers 250 square miles and, with a population of 5.3 million, is the eighth largest metropolis in the world. Its traffic problem is considered even worse than that of New York.   BRAZIL, LIFE WORLD LIBRARY

How did **Spain** *get its name?*

In the Sixth Century, the Phoenician settlers in Gadir (modern Cadiz) asked Carthage, a Phoenician colony in North Africa, for assistance in repulsing an attack by native tribes. The Carthaginians came and stayed, and gave the peninsula its name: Span or Spania, meaning "land of rabbits."   SPAIN, LIFE WORLD LIBRARY

What **species** *has the widest distribution?*

Aside from man, the housefly appears to be the most far ranging, being found almost everywhere except in the polar regions. Originally confined to tropical latitudes, it still flourishes most successfully at 77°F. but has been able to extend its range by spending the cooler seasons of the year in a dormant state and by adopting man's heated structures as its home. Similarly, the common cockroach, body louse, pharaoh ant and house mouse, plus a few other species—all also congeners with man—have invaded a diversity of environments.   ECOLOGY, LIFE NATURE LIBRARY

*How large a winter hoard does a **squirrel** gather?*

A single squirrel may hide away 20 or more bushels of food divided into
many small caches, although it may not find and eat a tenth of that reserve before spring. THE FOREST. LIFE NATURE LIBRARY

*How do astronomers measure the distance to a **star**?*

The only direct way to measure how far away the stars are is by a trick
of geometry known as parallax. Parallax is a measure of the amount by
which an object seems to move, in relation to its background, when an ob-
server looks at it from two different places. Astronomers learned to
measure the parallax of some 6,000 of the nearest stars by looking at
them during opposite seasons of the year when the earth's revolution
around the sun has given a base line 186 million miles long. Eventually, astronomers may be able to measure parallaxes of more distant stars, or
even remote galaxies, by taking advantage of the sun's own revolution
around the hub of the Milky Way. But since it takes 100 million years
for the sun to go halfway around the hub, the results will not be in for
some time. THE UNIVERSE. LIFE NATURE LIBRARY

Why does a *star* twinkle?

The earth's own atmosphere is the chief obstacle to a clear view of the heavens. The reason stars twinkle and the images of planets shimmer is that the air swirls and roils like a stormy sea. Astronomers have tried to escape the interference by building observatories on mountaintops, above most of the turbulence and clouds. Even up there, absorption of light by ozone, carbon dioxide and water in the atmosphere blocks the scientists' observation of most infrared and ultraviolet radiation. Only when the first automatically guided telescopes were sent aloft on balloons in 1959— and later by satellite—were these limitations partly overcome.

PLANETS. LIFE SCIENCE LIBRARY

How did the designations *"starboard"* and *"port"* originate?

The Viking ships were fitted with one rudder—a long, straight blade, controlled by a tiller slotted at right angles into the rudderhead. The tiller was located on the right side of the stern, a placement which explains how the term "starboard," a corruption of "steer board," or steering side, came to mean the right side of the ship. The term "port" was applied to the left side because the crew always tied up the ship in port with this rudderless side against the quay. "Larboard," another term for the left side, came from the word *ladeborde*, the loading side, where cargo was received. SHIPS. LIFE SCIENCE LIBRARY

How does a *stereo* phonograph work?

Different kinds of grooves make the difference between monaural and stereophonic phonograph records. Because a monaural system has only one sound track, both sides of the groove are the same and a single sound stream is produced by the needle's vibrations. On a stereophonic record each side of the groove carries a separate message. The needle feeds the two tracks into separate speakers.

SOUND AND HEARING. LIFE SCIENCE LIBRARY

How many people took part in the *stock-buying spree* of 1928-1929?

There were about 600,000 margin, presumably speculative, accounts, in which a customer put up only part of the purchase money, securing a loan from his broker to cover the rest. Since only a relatively small number of individuals were speculating, the inflation in security values may have been brought on as much through the idiocy of suckers at the very top of the financial community as through the avidity of suckers from the hinterland. WAR. BOOM AND BUST. THE LIFE HISTORY OF THE UNITED STATES

Why are there two *stock exchanges* in New York?

Speculators and freelance brokers who were not members of the New York Stock Exchange clung to its fringes, trading in the street at the "curb market." Outdoor trading, rain or shine, was more chaotic and sometimes—as during the Civil War—busier than indoor trading. By 1912 the New York Curb Exchange had been organized. In 1921 its members also moved indoors, and in 1953 they chose the more dignified name of the American Stock Exchange. THE GATEWAY STATES. TIME-LIFE LIBRARY OF AMERICA

Who built the *Suez Canal?*

The Suez Canal was officially started in 1854 when an imaginative French diplomat, Ferdinand de Lesseps, obtained a concession from Egypt authorizing him to form a company to build it. The work, carried out primarily by French engineers and Egyptian laborers, began in 1859 and was completed in 1869 at a cost of $287 million. Before the Arab-Israeli war of 1967 the Canal transported roughly half of the commerce between Europe and the Far East. THE ARAB WORLD, LIFE WORLD LIBRARY

What is the Japanese sport of *sumó*?

The oldest form of Japanese wrestling, *sumó* calls itself "the national sport." To the expert, *sumó* is a sport of infinite subtlety, each of its holds and throws being as carefully defined and documented as the points of a show dog. The basic rules are nevertheless simple. The contestant may take a grip on the upper part of his opponent's body or on the stiff silk loincloth; he wins a match if he forces his opponent from the ring or makes any part of his opponent's body except the soles of his feet touch the ground. The preliminary ritual of *sumó* is slow and complex; the average time of an actual match is something like 10 seconds.

JAPAN, LIFE WORLD LIBRARY

Is there a **Swiss army**?

The Swiss do not have an army; they are an army. Switzerland is the only country in the world where the entire able-bodied male population is under constant alert to mobilize. Every man is a soldier from his 20th to his 60th year. SWITZERLAND, LIFE WORLD LIBRARY

What's the attraction of a **Swiss bank account**?

The Swiss love to husband other people's money almost as much as their own, and they have never cared particularly whose money it is. Nazi fortunes were secured behind the red-geranium window boxes of the great banks, and Latin American dictators have stashed away their piles there. A depositor in a Swiss bank can arrange to have his account identified by number and the number known only to himself and a handful of top bank officials. SWITZERLAND, LIFE WORLD LIBRARY

Why is the **Swiss president** so anonymous?

Switzerland changes presidents every year, and many citizens never bother to remember the name of the present incumbent. The Swiss mistrust people who rise too far above the herd. Heredity and wealth are political detriments for a Swiss. The president, who is chairman of the Federal Council (somewhat like our Cabinet) and serves as head of state, rents a modest apartment, pays the salary of his single maid himself and is expected to ride to work on the streetcar. SWITZERLAND, LIFE WORLD LIBRARY

What were the first symposiums?

At Athenian banquets in ancient Greece, guests concentrated on the food; sparkling conversations were a feature of the symposium, or drinking session, that followed. Here the most important man was the symposiarch, chosen by lot or a throw of the dice, who took charge of everything. He decided how much water would be mixed with the wine, called in the entertainers—dancing girls, acrobats and magicians—and set the guests to entertaining one another. A symposiarch like the philosopher Socrates might pose brain-crunching riddles, but less intellectual symposiarchs would assign a bald-headed man to comb his hair, a stutterer to orate or an ardent fellow to race around the room with the flute girl in his arms. CLASSICAL GREECE, GREAT AGES OF MAN

T is for tangos, traffic hazards and twins

*Where did the **tango** originate?*

Its origin seems to be dual—both Argentine and European. Combining elements borrowed from the Buenos Aires slums and from Spain, the tango first became popular at the beginning of the 20th Century. At that time it was urban and unrespectable, sung in the sleazy bars of La Boca, the dockside district of Buenos Aires where the bohemians and the working class mixed, and where it was picked up by smart young men sowing their wild oats. Many of these young men subsequently went to Paris, where they introduced the tango to higher social circles. Thus given a social cachet, it returned to Argentina about 1917 in its modern form and remained the most popular music in the region for more than 30 years. It has been on the wane in recent years as Argentina has turned to the pop tunes of Liverpool, London and New York, as well as to earlier and more authentically native music.

THE RIVER PLATE REPUBLICS. LIFE WORLD LIBRARY

Does Russia have a sales *tax*?

Russia has financed its industrialization partly with forced loans but chiefly by selling consumer goods at enormous markups—a form of enforced sales tax. To this day, if a Soviet woman needs, say, four yards of plain, unbleached white cotton to make a new work smock, she may have to pay as much as 70 cents a yard for it—or $2.80. Since cost figures are usually secret in the Soviet economy, she does not know that the cotton cost the government only 20 cents a yard to produce, or 80 cents for the four yards she purchased. The remaining two dollars that she had to pay is simply a tax and probably will be used to finance a new factory or, perhaps, a new rocket to the moon. RUSSIA, LIFE WORLD LIBRARY

Was William *Tell* a real man or a mythical one?

Tell probably never existed. Nevertheless, his supposed birthplace in Bürglen is marked by a chapel. Frescoed shrines stand in Altdorf, where he is said to have shot the apple from his son's head; near Flüelen, where he escaped from an Austrian boat; in the Hohle Gasse (hollow lane) near Küssnacht, where he ambushed and shot the villainous Gessler; and on the bank of the Schächen River, where a stone cross indicates the depths in which he is supposed to have drowned. SWITZERLAND, LIFE WORLD LIBRARY

In what *temperature range* do humans do their best work?

Space researchers have found that a man with no insulation can very briefly endure temperatures of up to 500°F. But simple endurance is not enough. Tests have shown that humans can perform tasks efficiently within a spread of only 35°—from about 50° to 85° above zero. Below 50°, limbs stiffen; above 85°, mental activity becomes sluggish.

MAN AND SPACE, LIFE SCIENCE LIBRARY

Why does the Second Law of *Thermodynamics* doom the universe?

The essence of the law is this: Heat will not flow, of its own accord, from a cold place to a hot one. Without hills of temperature (i.e., places where it is hotter than other places), heat can do no work. There is a process of heat erosion in the universe that tends to level out temperature; this insidious leveler is heat loss. The conclusion of this losing game causes us to face a day when all the energy in the universe has been converted to heat and all of this heat has been evenly distributed throughout the universe. This does not mean that the universe necessarily will grow very cold. It could, instead, become either lukewarm or white hot. The point is that it will be the same temperature everywhere. And this means no more work can be done.

ENERGY. LIFE SCIENCE LIBRARY

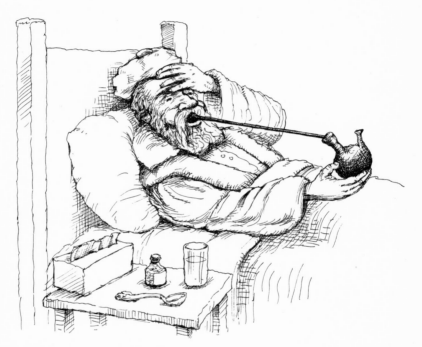

*Who invented the **thermometer**?*

The early Greeks knew that air expands as it grows warmer and contracts with cooling. Galileo Galilei, applying this principle, invented the thermometer about 1600. His "thermoscope" consisted of a thin glass tube a foot and a half long. It was blown into an egg-sized bulb at one end but was open at the other. Galileo warmed the bulb in his hands, then placed the open end in water. As the bulb cooled, the air inside contracted, and water pushed part way up the tube. From this level, the column of water rose or fell with every change of temperature. With the addition of an arbitrary scale, it became a crude thermometer.

WEATHER. LIFE SCIENCE LIBRARY

What creates a **tidal wave**?

Tidal waves, or tsunamis, are caused by world-shaking earthquakes and volcanic eruptions beneath the sea. They cross the ocean in the form of low waves, so low in fact that ships at sea often do not know that a tsunami is passing. They flash through the water at jet-plane speed, averaging about 450 miles per hour. Individual waves travel more than 15 minutes apart, and the first one is not necessarily the worst. When they approach shallow water, they rise to overwhelming heights and hit with pulverizing force. They have been known to rise 60 feet on flat, low-lying shores and more than a hundred feet at the head of V-shaped inlets.

THE SEA, LIFE NATURE LIBRARY

How did nautical **timekeeping** by "bells" originate?

During the great Age of Discovery of the 15th and 16th Centuries, pilots and mariners had few mechanical timepieces of any description. They kept track of time as best they could by means of half-hour sandglasses. Every half hour, as the last of the sand ran out, a man on watch turned it over; he struck a bell for each turn since the beginning of the watch, usually a period of four hours. The practice still survives on shipboard and explains timekeeping by "bells"—one bell for 12:30, two bells for 1 o'clock, three bells for 1:30, and so on, up to eight bells for 4 o'clock, when a new watch begins and the count starts over.

SHIPS, LIFE SCIENCE LIBRARY

How valuable is land in **Tokyo**?

Recently the selling price of property fronting on the exclusive Ginza was estimated to be $18 million per acre. Choice locations in Manhattan bring only half that amount. Even in some residential areas around Tokyo a price of $38,000 an acre is not unusual. JAPAN, LIFE WORLD LIBRARY

What causes a **tornado**?

The most violent winds on earth are those that spin in the funnel cloud of a tornado. Moving as fast as 500 miles per hour, these deadly coils of wind pack a doubly destructive power: their winds at the outer edges can hurl aside almost anything in their path; within the funnel, the air pressure is so low that houses explode from the pressure of expanding air inside them. Tornadoes, most of which occur in the U.S. Midwest, are bred by colliding air masses. According to one theory, fast-moving cold, dry air overruns moist, tropical air— instead of wedging under, as usually happens—creating a tremendous imbalance. The warm air rushes upward, sometimes at 200 miles per hour. Air flowing in from the sides gives the updrafts a twist. The vortex begins to spin, accompanied by rain or hail and almost continuous flashes of lightning. Tornadoes travel at up to 40 miles per hour and usually last only a few minutes. But those minutes can be catastrophic. WEATHER. LIFE SCIENCE LIBRARY

*What unique **traffic hazard** plagues the Dutch?*

An average of 50 cars a year drive into the Amsterdam canals, a problem that is the responsibility of a special branch of the Amsterdam municipal police called the *grachtenvissers* (canal fishermen). The *grachtenvissers* also dispense information on what to do when trapped in a sinking automobile: stay calm, keep car windows closed; when water stops rising in car, open windows and swim out. THE LOW COUNTRIES. LIFE WORLD LIBRARY

*When was **train travel** introduced into the U.S.?*

The first railroad engine to run in the U.S., the *Stourbridge Lion*, managed a modest 10 miles per hour in a trial near Honesdale, Pennsylvania, on August 8, 1829.   WHEELS, LIFE SCIENCE LIBRARY

*Can you tell the age of a **tree** by counting stump rings?*

In temperate climate, a single ring of light and dark wood is usually added each year—but sometimes more than one ring is produced in a growing season, or sometimes no ring at all. If a tree loses most of its leaves from a severe insect attack or drought, it begins producing dense wood and thus completes a ring. Then if a new crop of leaves grows again that same season, another ring will be formed. In a very dry year the tree might not grow at all, and no ring would be added that year.

THE FOREST, LIFE NATURE LIBRARY

*How large was ancient **Troy**?*

All the facts of the *Iliad* of Homer and the *Aeneid* of Virgil are accurate. Mount Ida, still forested, rises behind Troy. The island of Tenedos, which concealed the treacherous Greek fleet when the wooden horse was placed before Troy's gates, still exists. Even the winds to which Homer so often alludes in his stock phrase, "wind-swept Troy," blow endlessly from the Aegean. What is inaccurate is the puffing up of fantasy in the minds of readers. Troy, Priam's proud capital, long-sought goal reached over the wine-dark sea by swift-footed Achilles, ambitious Agamemnon and crafty Odysseus, was, alas, not an imperial city but a village of some seven acres. And the Trojan War must have been merely a bloodstained squabble between clans. The cruelty of Achilles in dragging Hector's body around and around the city walls under the eyes of the Trojan women is entirely credible, something a village ruffian could easily do with his rival, given a chariot and two horses.   TURKEY, LIFE WORLD LIBRARY

*By what method did the famous **Tweed Ring** of the 19th Century steal money from the City of New York?*

A typical operation of Tammany Hall, the Democratic machine that ruled New York City under William M. ("Boss") Tweed after the Civil

War, was the construction of a courthouse for more than $11 million when the actual value was three million; one plasterer was paid $133,000 for two days of work, and the thermometers for the building cost $7,500. The total cost to the city of various Tweed Ring operations was estimated at $200 million over six years.

THE UNION RESTORED, THE LIFE HISTORY OF THE UNITED STATES

*What are the chances of having **twins**?*

A number of factors have been discovered that increase the likelihood that a woman will bear fraternal twins. Age is a major determinant. A woman in her late thirties is more likely to give birth to twins than one who is still in her teens. Prior experience of motherhood also seems to increase the possibility of having twins. American girls from 15 to 19 who have never had babies before have one chance in 200 of giving birth to twins. With women 35 to 39 who have already borne a number of children the chances go up to one in 50. It is also thought that genetic characteristics play an important part in producing multiple births. The tendency to twinning seems to run in females of the same family, being passed on from mother to daughter.   GROWTH, LIFE SCIENCE LIBRARY

U is for "Uncle Tom's Cabin" and uranium

How successful was "Uncle Tom's Cabin"?

In 1852 there occurred the most effective single abolitionist blow at slavery, and it was struck by the hand of a woman. Harriet Beecher Stowe embodied the reforming religious spirit of New England, its lofty moral sense and its terrible zeal. Urged on by her family and her own inclinations, she decided to write something about slavery. The result was a serial story in a religious magazine that kept growing until it became a novel. Published under the title *Uncle Tom's Cabin; or, Life Among the Lowly,* it was an instantaneous and sensational success. The first printing sold out in two days, new printings could not keep up with the orders, and by the end of 1852 over 300,000 copies had been sold. Even then the demand did not cease, and dramatized as a play the book reached a still wider audience. Published abroad, it sold even better—more than one million copies in the British Empire alone.

THE UNION SUNDERED, THE LIFE HISTORY OF THE UNITED STATES

How long did it take to draft the *U.S. Constitution*?

The pace of the Federal Convention in 1787 is impressive evidence of the ability of the delegates to come to terms with one another and to get work done. The convention opened on May 25. By July 26 a basic plan for the Constitution had been adopted and sent to a Committee of Detail. That committee swiftly presented a draft version, which was debated clause by clause from August 6 until September 10, when the Constitution was agreed upon and referred to a Committee of Style for finishing touches. The Committee of Style presented the final draft for approval on September 12. On September 17 the convention happily adjourned, as Washington noted in his diary, "to the City Tavern." There the delegates dined contentedly together.

THE MAKING OF A NATION, THE LIFE HISTORY OF THE UNITED STATES

Is *uranium* rare?

With the explosion of the first atomic bomb over the New Mexico desert in 1945, uranium—the basic ingredient of nuclear power and weapons —suddenly became the most sought-after metal of the nuclear age. As metals go, it is neither very rare nor particularly glamorous. Because it never occurs in a pure state, and seldom in heavy concentration, vast amounts of ore must be found, mined and refined in a long, costly process to produce small quantities of the final product.

THE EARTH, LIFE NATURE LIBRARY

V is for vineyards, vision and volcanoes

How healthful is a vegetarian diet?

Vegetarians often point to George Bernard Shaw's long life—he died at the age of 94—as evidence that their custom is conducive to good health, strength and longevity. Nutritionists know of no basis for these claims, although the practice need not be harmful. By forgoing meat, the vegetarian deprives himself of the primary source of high-quality protein. He makes it harder to obtain his nutrition. But theoretically he can get all the essential nutrients from a meatless diet—even if he abstains from eggs and milk as well. To do so he must select his vegetable foods carefully and know his nutritional requirements. The most elusive nutrient for the strict vegetarian is Vitamin B_{12}. It can be synthesized by chemical fermentation processes, but otherwise comes almost entirely from animal sources. While the vegetable diet may be questionable nutritionally, its ethical basis helps to explain its widespread acceptance.

FOOD AND NUTRITION, LIFE SCIENCE LIBRARY

What was the first self-propelled *vehicle* used for?

The first self-contained, mechanically driven road vehicle was designed in 1769. A steam-powered tractor for pulling cannon, it was a top-heavy, three-wheeled carriage whose boiler awkwardly protruded over the single front wheel; it looked, contemporaries said, like "a whisky still on a wheelbarrow." Its maximum speed was four miles per hour, and at that it had to pause every block or so to build up steam. Its builder, a French Army captain named N. J. Cugnot, ultimately drove the cart into a stone wall. Historians report that he was promptly thrown into jail—the first known traffic offender.   MACHINES, LIFE SCIENCE LIBRARY

How long is a day on *Venus?*

Venus' retrograde rotation is very slow. It turns on its axis about once in 250 earth days. Since its orbit around the sun takes 224.7 days, the combination of the two motions makes sunrise take place on Venus at intervals of about 118 earth days.   PLANETS, LIFE SCIENCE LIBRARY

Did the *Vikings* travel east as well as west?

Yes; many of these merchant adventurers penetrated as far into the continents of Europe and Asia as their western brethren traveled across the At-

lantic. The very name of Russia is derived from them, for they were
known as the Rhos or Rus. The word applies only to Swedish Vikings
in Russia, not to the Swedes in their homeland, and the theory is that it derived from the word *rodr,* the rowing road. In 839 Louis the Pious, son
of Charlemagne, received an embassy from the Byzantine Emperor that
included men of Swedish origin calling themselves Rhos.

SCANDINAVIA, LIFE WORLD LIBRARY

How valuable is land in the vineyards of France?

A vineyard like the Romanée-Conti in Burgundy, which comprises only
four and a half acres, is nearly as valuable as it would be if the land were located in downtown Chicago. FRANCE, LIFE WORLD LIBRARY

How did the Virgin Islands get their name?

The Virgin Islands were discovered by Christopher Columbus during
his second voyage in 1493. Their name comes from the legend of St. Ur-
sula, who is said to have made a pilgrimage to Rome accompanied by 10,-
999 virgins and to have been martyred, with all her companions, by
Attila the Hun. To Columbus' crew on that voyage it appeared that
they were sailing among thousands of islands, and someone, perhaps Columbus himself, remembered the legend and named the islands the
Virgins. THE WEST INDIES, LIFE WORLD LIBRARY

What size is a virus?

Viruses are so small that they approach molecular dimensions. Some
2,000 average-sized human cells placed side by side would extend about
an inch; a single one of these cells could hold more than 60 million polio
viruses. THE CELL, LIFE SCIENCE LIBRARY

How good is man's vision?

Man's visual system is closest to those of his immediate ancestors, the tree-
climbing animals, whose eyes are adapted to focus rapidly as they swing
from limb to limb. The eyes face forward in their heads, so that their owners can look at a point with both eyes at once. They can also aim and
focus to bring the images of the two eyes together, so that the picture

they get is three-dimensional—and in sharp outline. Man's eyes have traded certain advantages for others: they are versatile and highly accurate, but less acute than a hawk's and less wide-sweeping than a deer's. They are not ideally suited for seeing underwater, nor are they as efficient at night as an owl's. Yet with all the compromises, they retain a staggering degree of adaptability and precision. They are capable of extremely rapid movement, of instantaneous shifts in focus from a book in hand to a distant star, of adapting to bright or dim light, of distinguishing colors, and of estimating distance, size and direction of movement.

LIGHT AND VISION, LIFE SCIENCE LIBRARY

Do *volcanoes* do any good?

They are indispensable to life. It is quite probable that volcanoes are responsible for the air we breathe and the water we drink. For, along with the noxious gases they exhale during eruptions, they send out the basic ingredients of the earth's atmosphere, such as nitrogen, hydrogen and carbon dioxide. In addition, there are a number of localized benefits conferred by these fire-breathing mountains: therapeutic hot springs in many countries, free steam heat for schools in Iceland and Japan, abundant hot water for laundries in New Zealand, electric power in Italy, and—the most widespread—fertility to the soil all around them.

THE MOUNTAINS, LIFE NATURE LIBRARY

How does a mountain *vole* control overpopulation?

The fecundity of this small rodent is overwhelming. A female vole becomes sexually mature at five weeks and thereafter may deliver litters of up to eight offspring every three weeks. Eagles, hawks, foxes, weasels all take their toll, but clearly no predator can eat that many voles. As a result, the voles would live in constant danger of self-extermination through overpopulation if they were not subject to an extraordinary regulator. The number of voles in a given area builds up very rapidly. Then, quite suddenly, instead of going about their regular business, they become nervous and agitated and spend most of their time wildly shredding grasses and sedges. Breeding is forgotten and, since the life expectancy of the vole is just under one year on the average, in a very short time the population drops to less than 1 per cent of what it had been.

THE MOUNTAINS, LIFE NATURE LIBRARY

W is for wakes, weather forecasts and white noise

Are wakes still held in Ireland?

The old traditional Irish wake, with several nights of drinking, reminiscing and storytelling, is now only a remembrance of the past in Ireland. The Church has discouraged it in recent years because it became too social, too much of an expensive hardship for many bereaved families and the butt of too many jokes. The present procedure is to wake the body for only one night at home. Then it is taken to the church, where there is a brief service with a rosary on the second evening, with the funeral on the following morning.

IRELAND, LIFE WORLD LIBRARY

Where did Wales get its name?

"Wales" is derived from the Anglo-Saxon word for "foreigners" and was conferred upon the country by the English. The national name is "Cymru," meaning "countryman" or "friend."

BRITAIN, LIFE WORLD LIBRARY

What American war had the highest casualty rate?

The Civil War was the most terrible that Americans have ever fought. The casualties were appalling—nearly one out of every four men in service died of disease, wounds or other causes. During much of the war 18th Century tactics contended with modern weapons, and often in dense woodland. Infantrymen often advanced shoulder to shoulder, Napoleonic-style, into a butchering fire of accurate new rifled muskets, or found themselves pinned down in a wild tangle by an invisible foe.

THE UNION RESTORED, THE LIFE HISTORY OF THE UNITED STATES

What continent has never had a major war?

Australia is the only big nation that was founded without internal war or revolution. Certainly, Australian soldiers have won high honor in battles overseas. But at home, except for minor skirmishes, peace has reigned from the beginning. AUSTRALIA AND NEW ZEALAND, LIFE WORLD LIBRARY

*How large an army did George **Washington** lead into battle?*

Although there were over 200,000 enlistments during the Revolutionary War, General Washington in fact never had more than 8,000 Continental regulars in a single battle. American troops were drawn from a colonial population of more than two million, of which some 500,000 were Tory sympathizers. Opposed to them were General Gage's 4,000 men, to whom the British added as many as 55,000 more soldiers, including about 30,000 German-speaking mercenaries, and many American Tories and Indians. THE MAKING OF A NATION, THE LIFE HISTORY OF THE UNITED STATES

*Did George **Washington** warn against entangling alliances?*

In his Farewell Address, which he sent to the newspapers, President Washington warned against permitting political parties and the dissension they stirred up to weaken the unity so necessary for the nation's survival. He cautioned also against permanent alliances with other countries and instead recommended "temporary alliances for extraordinary emergencies." He did not use the phrase "entangling alliances" often credited to him; Thomas Jefferson later did so in his First Inaugural Address.

THE GROWING YEARS, THE LIFE HISTORY OF THE UNITED STATES

How much water is used daily, per capita, in the U.S.?

Economic development, more than any other single factor, increases water use. In the underdeveloped nations, the per capita water consumption for all purposes—domestic, agricultural and industrial—is about 10 gallons a day. In the U.S., it is about 1,800 gallons—of which about 1,700 gallons are used for agriculture and industry.

WATER, LIFE SCIENCE LIBRARY

Is the earth's water supply decreasing?

Water's behavior is steadfast: the total supply neither grows nor diminishes. It is believed to be almost precisely the same now as it was three billion years ago. Endlessly recycled, water is used, disposed of, purified and used again. Last night's potatoes may have boiled in what was, ages ago, the bath water of Archimedes. But while the total supply of water is not a concern, its distribution and management, of course, are.

WATER, LIFE SCIENCE LIBRARY

Can wealth be inherited in Russia?

Income taxes have never been higher than 13 per cent in Soviet Russia, so members of the elite can look forward to keeping most of their money. Though Marx inveighed against inherited wealth, there is no inheritance tax in the Soviet Union beyond a simple probate fee. Thus the very rich can guarantee that their children will also be rich.

RUSSIA, LIFE WORLD LIBRARY

How accurate are weather forecasts?

When the Weather Bureau first began using computer technology in 1955, an improvement in accuracy, "slight but significant," was noted almost immediately. Today 12- to 18-hour forecasts are considered 85 per cent accurate; forecasts up to 36 hours in advance are correct about 75 per cent of the time. Though general weather conditions for about a week in advance can be forecast with some degree of usefulness, it is still beyond the capabilities of science to make detailed predictions for more than about three days in advance. WEATHER, LIFE SCIENCE LIBRARY

How dangerous is excess weight?

The dangers of overeating were recognized more than half a century ago, when actuarial studies by life-insurance companies indicated that fat policyholders were poor risks. By now there are mountains of statistics that establish beyond any question that overweight people do not live as long, on the average, as slimmer ones. A table prepared by the Metropolitan Life Insurance Company, showing the mortality rates among men, indicates that as little as 10 per cent in excess poundage increases the likelihood of death by 13 per cent. And the risk increases with every additional pound of weight. Men who are 20 per cent overweight have a 25 per cent greater chance of dying prematurely than do those of normal weight; those who are 30 per cent overweight have a 42 per cent greater chance. The figures for women are not quite so dramatic, but they are equally disturbing. FOOD AND NUTRITION, LIFE SCIENCE LIBRARY

*Where was the **wheel** invented?*

An unknown Sumerian on the fertile delta of the Tigris and Euphrates Rivers, some time in the Third Millennium B.C., produced what must surely be man's greatest single technological achievement. He made a wheel. Precisely who he was or how he planned to use it will never be known. He may have been a warrior putting together his first war chariot. Or he may have been a mourner providing a smoother ride for some particularly esteemed corpse. The earliest record of a vehicular wheel is a sketch made by an accountant in Sumer about 3500 B.C. The vehicle was apparently a funeral wagon, a bizarre contraption with an undercarriage that swooped up in front like the runners of old-fashioned Hans Brinker ice skates, indicating that this wagon may have been an immediate offspring of the land sledge. Underneath, there were two pairs of unmistakable wheels. WHEELS, LIFE SCIENCE LIBRARY

Who designed the **White House?**

Winner in the government-sponsored competition for a Presidential residence was a Georgian design by James Hoban, who later supervised the building's construction. Congress voted to give a prize award of either $500 or a gold medal for the design. Hoban, who had to feed a wife and 10 children, chose the $500. THE GROWING YEARS, THE LIFE HISTORY OF THE UNITED STATES

What is white noise?

Although a quiet office is certainly preferable to a noisy one, too much quiet can produce problems. In some instances, acoustical engineers have recommended the deliberate introduction of background sound through ventilating and air-conditioning systems. The background sound preferred by most acoustical engineers, known technically as "white noise," is a blend of audible frequencies over a wide range. To the layman, it most nearly resembles the soft rush of escaping steam. White noise can be used not only to convert disturbing silence into a controlled quiet but also to mask noises that would otherwise be distracting.

SOUND AND HEARING, LIFE SCIENCE LIBRARY

What are the **Windward Islands** windward of?

To sailors, "windward" means the direction from which the wind is coming, "leeward" the direction toward which it is blowing. The trade wind blows over the West Indies from an easterly direction. The northern British islands were originally named the Leewards because they lay to leeward of the important colony of Barbados. The southern group, which lies to windward of the Spanish-held mainland, was for that reason named the Windwards.

THE WEST INDIES, LIFE WORLD LIBRARY

What was the first U.S. **women's college?**

The first college-level institution for women was the Mount Holyoke Female Seminary, which Mary Lyon opened in South Hadley, Massachusetts, in 1837. Mount Holyoke was founded with $27,000 collected from no fewer than 1,800 people in 90 towns. Mrs. Lyon ran the college by spartan rules. The girls could sleep as long as they liked on Thanksgiving—provided they got to breakfast at 8.

THE SWEEP WESTWARD, THE LIFE HISTORY OF THE UNITED STATES

How long can a **woodpecker** peck?

A woodpecker is an animated chisel. It digs into wood by knocking out small chips with its bill. It grasps the tree with its claws, props itself with its stiff tail, then bends back the upper part of its body to put force behind each swing. It can beat its head against wood 20 times a second, in uninterrupted bursts of almost an hour, and dig holes more than a foot deep into the heartwood of a living tree. In the process, it sets up vibrations in its skull that would probably kill any other bird.

THE FOREST, LIFE NATURE LIBRARY

*Did the U.S. win **World War I** for the Allies?*

Without the foodstuffs, munitions, money and other essentials that the American economy supplied, the Allies almost certainly would not have held out so long as they did. On the other hand, the tally of dead and wounded—6,161,000 French, 3,190,000 British, 7,143,000 Germans, 349,000 Americans—proved that the worst of the war had been waged before America joined in. War, Boom and Bust. The Life History of the United States

*Were Axis efforts coordinated in **World War II**?*

There was little teamwork or amity in the Axis, and Germany was caught completely by surprise by the Pearl Harbor attack. Japan had no affection for the racist Nazis, while Hitler reputedly remarked after the fall of Singapore that he would gladly send 20 divisions to help repel the yellow man. New Deal and Global War. The Life History of the United States

How did *World War II* end?

On the morning of August 6, 1945, an atomic bomb was dropped on the city of Hiroshima. Almost 68,000 were killed, with as many injured. Nevertheless, Japan did not sue for peace. On August 9, a few hours after Russia had declared war on Japan, a second atomic bomb was exploded over Nagasaki; 38,000 were killed. Even then, Japanese leaders balked at surrender. The Emperor had to override his two chief military advisers in order to accept surrender terms.

NEW DEAL AND GLOBAL WAR, THE LIFE HISTORY OF THE UNITED STATES

How does a *wound* heal?

When you cut your finger, a fluid discharge covers the exposed region and forms a film over it. The film includes fibrous strands, which stretch across the wound and probably provide guidelines for the migrating cells that form the new tissue. After the formation of the fibrous film, some skin cells become detached and are free to wander about. This is a controlled migration of individuals—something like the movement of a herd of animals. Deeper-lying cells migrate to replace those that were destroyed by the cut. New capillaries are formed. At the same time, other cells advance from the edges of the wound, perhaps following the fibrous guidelines, and bridge the surface of the wound. Bit by bit, the tissue is restored to normal. There is a final act in the healing process. The tissues of a wound not only grow when needed, they stop growing as soon as healing is completed. THE CELL, LIFE SCIENCE LIBRARY

Y is for yak, yellow journalism and yoga

Of what use is the yak?

The key to life for the people of the high Tibetan plateau is that shaggy, ill-tempered relative of the buffalo called the yak. As an all-purpose, high-altitude friend to man, the yak beats even the llama. One does not milk a llama. But the yak furnishes meat, wool, milk, butter, hide for tents, and dung for fuel. What's more, a tamed, native ox can even be saddled for transport.

THE MOUNTAINS. LIFE NATURE LIBRARY

How did "yellow journalism" get its name?

Funny cartoons in color appeared in the 1890s, when the Sunday editions of the New York *World* displayed no fewer than eight pages of primitive "funnies," four in color. One such cartoon was entitled "Hogan's Alley," featuring the rowdy antics of a number of urchins, one of them dressed in a violent yellow garment imperfectly resembling a nightshirt.

When Hearst's *Journal* stole the Yellow Kid's cartoonist from Pulitzer's *World,* both papers ran rival Yellow Kid comics. During the ensuing "comics war" between these ruthless competitors, the term "yellow journalism" was coined. REACHING FOR EMPIRE. THE LIFE HISTORY OF THE UNITED STATES

What is yoga?

"Yoga," deriving from the same root as the English "yoke," carries the same double meaning: to harness or discipline (under the yoke) and to unite (yoke with). The word is loosely applied to programs and techniques that lead toward union with God. More specifically, and as it is generally understood in the West, yoga refers to a technique of physical and mental self-discipline achieved through various exercises and postures. The practitioner is called a yogi. INDIA. LIFE WORLD LIBRARY